DISCOVERING LIFE ON EARTH

DISCOVERING LIFE ON EARTH

A NATURAL HISTORY

David Attenborough

COLLINS

Picture research by Diane Rich

Editor: Ingrid Selberg
Art Editor: Enid Fairhead
Assistant: Caroline Hill
Production: Emma Bradford

First published in this revised edition
by William Collins Sons & Co Ltd 1981

Reprinted 1982

Original edition of *Life on Earth* first
published 1979 by William Collins Sons & Co Ltd
14 St James's Place London SW1
and the British Broadcasting Corporation
35 Marylebone High Street London W1

© David Attenborough Productions Ltd 1979 and 1981

ISBN 0 00 195147-5 (hardback)
ISBN 0 00 195148-3 (paperback)

Set in Monophoto Bembo by Servis Filmsetting Ltd Manchester
Colour origination by Culver Graphics Ltd
Printed and bound in Hong Kong by South China Printing Co

Contents

Introduction

The variety of animals is amazing. Even when you look at just one small plot of land – your own back garden, perhaps – you find a great number of animals with very different kinds of bodies. Some are large and familiar – the birds, which have warm blood and feathers and lay eggs; and the cats, which chase them and also have warm blood, but are covered in fur and produce, not eggs in shells, but live kittens. There are a great number of other creatures too, that are more easily overlooked – millipedes curled up underneath stones with a hundred or so legs; eight-legged spiders crouched beside their webs waiting to catch creatures with six legs, such as flies, ants, beetles or butterflies; and beneath, worms that do not have any legs at all, munching their way through the soil.

Why should there be such an extraordinary number of different patterns for animal bodies? To answer this question, you have to look back to the beginnings of life and see how it has developed over the last 3,500 million years. That may sound an almost impossible job, but there are a lot of clues to suggest what happened. The most direct evidence is the remains of animals from the far distant past that we can find in the rocks as fossils. But a great deal can also be discovered by looking at living animals, watching what they do, examining the ways they are constructed, and working out, from their similarities and differences, which group is related to which.

From such evidence, scientists have been able to piece together the history of life in extraordinary detail. This long story was the subject of a series of television films, called *Life on Earth*, that was made for the BBC by a group of us whose names are at the back of this book. Later, I wrote a book based on those films and with the same title. Condensing 3,500 million years into a few hundred pages, describing groups of animals that contain many thousands of species in a single chapter, made it necessary to concentrate on the most important parts of the plot and to leave out a lot of the details. In this new version, I have shortened the text even more, but we have been able to show some of the detail by adding a large number of new pictures.

Our understanding of this immense history is by no means complete. Scientists know very well that there is a great deal that remains to be found out and a vast amount more that we will never know. But the story they have pieced together so far, incomplete though it still is, is one of endless fascination. As we follow it, we can see why that millipede has so many legs and why the slug has none, why frogs have to stay near water, why snakes are not found in the coldest parts of the world, why birds must be warm-blooded if they are to fly, and many many other things. Most important of all, perhaps, we can see that we ourselves are part of that natural world and are dependent on it, and that the natural world, since we have become the most powerful of all creatures, is now dependent upon us.

David Attenborough

1· The endless variety

It is not difficult to discover an unknown animal. Spend a day in a tropical jungle and you can collect hundreds of different kinds of small creatures. Moths, spiders, beetles, butterflies disguised as wasps, wasps shaped like ants, sticks that walk, leaves that open wings and fly. One of these creatures may well be new to science – though only a specialist could tell you which one.

The variety of animal and plant life is indeed vast and bewildering and ever since the beginning of science, people have wondered why this should be so. Over the centuries, many reasons have been suggested; one most widely accepted today was made by an English naturalist, Charles Darwin. In 1832 he was visiting Brazil. In a single day there he collected 68 different species of small beetles. He was astounded that there should be so many. An explanation of why this was so occurred to him three years later when his expedition arrived in the Galapagos Islands. These islands lie 1000 km from the coast of Ecuador, out in the Pacific. The Galapagos creatures Darwin saw looked very like those he had seen on the mainland, but they were slightly different. There were cormorants – black, long-necked diving birds like those that fly along Brazilian rivers, but their wings were so small that they were unable to fly. There were also

The strange animals of the Galapagos
A marine iguana (*above*) with a scarlet shore crab and (*below*) flightless cormorants.

The endless variety

large lizards called iguanas. Those on the continent climbed trees and ate leaves. Here on the islands, where there was little vegetation, one species fed on seaweed and clung to rocks among the waves with unusually long claws. There were tortoises, very similar to the mainland ones, except that these were many times bigger. Moreover, the tortoises on each island were slightly different. Those that lived on well-watered islands, where there was ground vegetation, had a front edge to their shells that curved gently upwards above their necks. But those that came from dry islands, where the only food was branches of cactus or leaves of trees, had a high peak to the front of their shells so that they could stretch their necks almost vertically upwards.

Darwin began to wonder if one species might, in time, change into another. Maybe, thousands of years ago, birds and reptiles from South America had reached the Galapagos on the rafts of vegetation that often float down the rivers and out to sea. Once there, they had changed, as generation followed generation, to suit their new homes.

The differences between them and their mainland cousins were

Giant tortoises from a well-watered island

10

only small, but if such changes had taken place, was it not possible that over many millions of years, many could add up to big changes. Maybe fish had developed muscular fins and crawled onto land to become amphibians. Maybe amphibians, in their turn, had developed watertight skins and become reptiles. But how did these changes come about? Darwin suggested that they were caused by a process he called 'natural selection'.

His argument was this. All individuals of the same species are not the same. For example, in one clutch of eggs from a giant tortoise, there may be some hatchlings which will develop longer necks than others because of factors inherited from their parents. In times of drought they will be able to reach leaves and so survive. Their brothers and sisters with shorter necks will starve and die. So those best fitted to their surroundings will be selected and survive. In turn, they will pass on their characteristics to their offspring. After a great number of generations, tortoises on the dry islands will have longer necks than those on the watered islands. And so one species will have given rise to another.

A giant tortoise from a dry island

HISTORY OF LIFE IN A YEAR
One day equals 10 million years

▼ *Millions of years ago*

Month	Myr	Event
DEC		Mammals appear
		The rocks at the top of the Grand Canyon were formed around this time
		Reptiles rule
	310	Backboned animals move onto land
NOV		The first backboned fish
		Life invades the land
	610	
OCT		Jellyfish and marine worms appear
		Sponges appear
	920	
SEPT		
	1220	
AUG		
	1530	
JULY		Protistans appear in the sea
	1840	
JUNE		The rocks in the bottom of the Grand Canyon were formed around this time
	2140	
MAY		
	2450	
APR		
	2750	
MAR		
	3060	
FEB		
	3340	Blue-greens appear in the sea
JAN		Life exists only as simple organisms like bacteria
	3650	

Darwin's theory remains the key to our understanding of the natural world. Since we have realized that plants and animals change or evolve, we have been able to piece together the history of animals and plants as they have developed and colonized the earth.

The direct evidence for this history lies in the earth's rocks. Most animals leave no trace of their existence after their death. But occasionally, one has a different fate. A reptile becomes stuck in a swamp and dies. Its body rots but its bones settle into the mud. Dead vegetation drifts to the bottom and covers them. As the centuries pass and more vegetation piles up, the deposit turns to peat. Changes in sea level may cause the swamp to be flooded and sand is deposited on top of the peat. Over great periods of time, the peat is pressed down and turned to coal. The reptile's bones still remain within it. Eventually they are turned to stone and they keep not only the outward shape that they had in life, but on occasion even their internal structure. So you can look at them through the microscope and see where the blood vessels and the nerves once were.

Scientists now have ways of measuring the age of many rocks chemically. But there is a much simpler way by which anyone can work out the *relative* age of rocks. If rocks lie in undisturbed layers, then the lower layer must be older than the upper. So by going deeper and deeper into the earth's crust, we can trace the history of animals back to their beginnings.

The deepest cleft that exists in the earth's surface is the Grand

	31		Modern man appears 35,000 years ago
	30	10	Ape-men appear
	29		
	28	30	
	27		Mammals greatly
	26	50	increase in numbers
	25		Dinosaurs
	24	70	disappear
	23		
	22	90	
	21		
	20	110	
DECEMBER	19		First flowering plants begin to
	18	130	bloom
	17		First birds take to the air
	16	150	Reptiles rule the land
	15		
	14	170	
	13		
	12	190	
	11		
	10	210	
	9		First mammals
	8	230	appear
	7		
	6	250	
	5		Trees begin to bear
	4	270	cones
	3		First reptiles
	2	290	appear
	1		
	30	310	
	29		Insects and
	28	330	amphibians develop on land
	27		Fish begin to leave
	26	350	the water
NOVEMBER	25		
	24	370	
	23		First animals
	22	390	move onto the land – millipedes
	21		First backboned
	20	410	fish appear in the sea
	19		
	18	430	
	17		Simple plants
	16	450	begin to grow on land

▲ *Days of the month*

Canyon in the western United States shown above. The rocks, through which the Colorado River has cut its way, still lie roughly horizontally.

A mule will carry you down it in an easy day's ride. The first rocks you pass are already some 200 million years old. There are no remains of mammals or birds in them, but there are traces of reptiles. Close by the side of the trail, you can see a line of tracks crossing the face of a sandstone boulder. They were made by a small lizard-like reptile, running across a beach. Other rocks at the same level elsewhere contains prints of fern leaves and the wings of insects.

Halfway down the Canyon, you come to 400 million-year-old limestones. There are no reptiles to be found here, but there are the bones of strange armoured fish. An hour or so later – and a 100 million years earlier – the rocks contain no sign of backboned animals of any kind. There are a few shells and worms that have left trails in what was the muddy sea floor. By three-quarters of the way down, there are no visible signs of life. When at last you reach the Colorado River, you are a vertical mile below the rim. The rocks here have been dated to the immense age of 2000 million years. Here you might hope to find evidence for the very beginning of life. But there are no fossils of any kind.

Is this because the rocks are so ancient that all such traces have been crushed from them? Or were the worms and shells which left their remains in the rocks above the very first kind of life to exist?

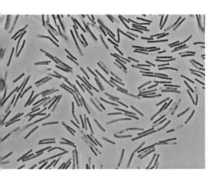

Bacteria magnified 1000 times
(*above*)

Fossil shells (*right*)
Some of these shells have been preserved complete. Others are represented by a cast of the shell or by a cast of its inside. All these can be called fossils.

The strange shapes in the rocks on the shores of Lake Superior

During the 1950s, scientists found answers to these questions in rocks of about the same age as those beside the Colorado River but 1500 km away on the shores of Lake Superior. Here there are layers of a special kind of flint called chert. In them are strange white circular patches about 1 m across. When researchers cut bits of these into thin sections and looked at them through the microscope, they saw tiny threads and circles very like the bodies of the simplest form of life existing today – algae and bacteria. Bacteria are tiny specks of living matter that can only be seen under the microscope. Algae are simple plants that are also very small but may grow into long threads and form tangles and carpets. So it seems from the fossil shapes in the chert that such things were among the earliest living beings to appear on earth.

Since those discoveries, other similar microscopic fossils have been found in Australia and South Africa that are about 3000 million years old. But if we want to consider how life arose, we have to look back a further 1000 million years to a time when the earth was completely lifeless and still cooling after its birth.

The planet then was very different from the one we live on today. The clouds of water vapour that had surrounded it had condensed to form seas, but they were still hot. We are not sure how the landmasses lay, but they certainly were not shaped like our modern continents. There were many volcanoes spewing ash and lava. The atmosphere was very thin and consisted of swirling clouds of gases. There was little or no oxygen. The mixture allowed ultraviolet rays from the sun to bathe the earth's surface with an intensity that would kill modern animals. Lightning bombarded the land and sea.

Laboratory experiments were made in the 1950s to discover what

A fossil ichthyosaurus (*left*)
The substance of the bones of this extinct swimming reptile has been replaced by stone so perfectly that the detailed structure of them can still be seen through a microscope.

A fossil fish (*below*)
This fish has left its bones in the rocks. The brown stain shows where its flesh once was.

would happen when such gases were treated with discharges of electricity and ultraviolet light. After only a week, the simple chemicals in the mixture began to combine to form complex ones, including sugars that are found today in the tissues of plants and animals. So it certainly seems possible that substances such as these could have formed in the seas of the earth at the very beginning of its history.

As the millions of years passed, these substances increased and began to interact with one another to form even more complex compounds. Eventually one substance appeared that was to lead to the further development of life. It is called de-oxy-ribo-nucleic acid, or DNA for short. Its structure enables it to do two important things. First, it can act as a blueprint for the manufacture of amino acids; and second, it can make copies of itself. These two characteristics of DNA are also those of living organisms such as bacteria. And bacteria, besides being among the simplest forms of life we know, are as we have seen, among the oldest fossils we have discovered. Some are over 3000 million years old.

Such vast ages are impossible to imagine, but we can get an idea of the relative length of the major stages in the history of life if we compare the entire span, from these first beginnings until today, with one year. Since we are unlikely yet to have discovered the oldest fossils of all, we can reckon that life started well before 3000 million years ago and as a rough guide we can let one day represent 10 million years. On such a calendar, the American chert fossils, which seemed so ancient when they were first discovered, are latecomers in the history of life, not appearing until the second week of August. In the Grand Canyon, the oldest worm trails were burrowed

The endless variety

A fossilized fern leaf (*right*)
Fossil leaves are seldom much more than a moulded shape and a thin film of carbon. But stems, roots and cones are sometimes turned to stone complete with their microscopic structure.

A fossil fly (*below*)
Insects are often preserved in amber, the fossilized lumps of resin that oozed out of tree trunks. This one, fell into mud and has, exceptionally, been preserved.

through the mud in the second week of November and the first fish appeared in the limestone seas a week later. The little lizard will have scuttled across the beach during the middle of December and humans did not appear until the evening of 31 December.

But we must return to January. The bacteria fed at first on the various substances that had formed in the seas over millions of years. But as they flourished, so this food must have become scarcer. Eventually some bacteria began to create such food for themselves. They used the energy of sunlight to help them build simple chemical molecules into bigger more complicated ones. This process is called photosynthesis. One of the ingredients it needs is hydrogen, a gas that is produced during volcanic eruptions. At this time, there were so many volcanoes that there was a lot of this gas around the earth. Later, however, bacteria-like forms appeared which got their hydrogen by breaking down the water. When that is done, what remains is oxygen. The living beings or organisms that did this are a little more complex than bacteria and are called blue-greens. The chemical they use to break down water in this way is a green substance called chlorophyll.

Blue-greens are still found today wherever there is constant moisture. You can often see mats of them, beaded with silver bubbles of oxygen, blanketing the bottoms of ponds. Over millions of years, the oxygen produced by blue-greens built up to form the kind of atmosphere that we know today. All animal life depends on it. We

need it not only to breathe but to protect us. Oxygen in the atmosphere forms a screen which cuts off most of the ultraviolet rays of the sun. These were the very rays which provided energy to produce the first complicated chemicals in the oceans. So the arrival of the blue-greens ruled out the possibility that life on earth could ever begin in the same way again.

Life remained at this stage of development for a vast period. Eventually, however, a further huge jump was made. You can find examples of the kind of organisms it produced in almost any patch of fresh water. A drop from a pond, viewed through a microscope, swarms with tiny organisms, some spinning and others crawling. As a group they are called the protista. Each of them has a body which is a single cell. That is, it is not divided by walls into a lot of separate parts. Even so, this single-celled body contains much more complex structures than any bacteria possess. The centre, or the nucleus, is full of DNA. This appears to be the organizing force of the cell. Elongated grains provide energy by using oxygen in much the same way as many bacteria do. Some contain chlorophyll and like blue-greens, use the energy of sunlight to make food. So each of these tiny organisms appears to be a committee of simpler ones. Some researchers believe that this is exactly what they are. It may be that one cell, which habitually fed by swallowing other particles, took some bacteria and blue-greens within it and these, instead of being digested, survived to collaborate in a communal life. We know from

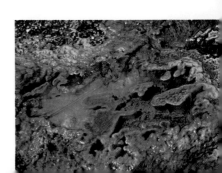

The endless variety

microscopic fossils that such protistans appeared about 1200 million years ago – say early September in the year of life.

Protistans reproduce by splitting into two, as bacteria do, but as their insides are much more complex, their division is a more elaborate business. Most of the separate structures, the members of the committee, themselves split. The DNA within the nucleus divides in a particularly complex way which ensures that each tiny particle of it is copied and that each daughter cell receives a duplicate set. There are, however, several other methods of reproduction practised by various protistans on occasions. The details vary. The essential feature of all of them is that new cells are produced which contain only half the normal amount of DNA. These cells are of two types – a large one, which usually does not move very much, and a smaller active one, driven by a beating thread called a flagellum. The first is called an egg and the second a sperm. This is the beginning of sexuality. These two types unite, so bringing the DNA in this new

Protistans from a freshwater pond (*Below*) a trumpet-shaped species magnified 300 times. (*Upper right*) a swiftly-swimming species. The lines of beating hairs on its body can be clearly seen. There are bigger ones around its mouth. (*Lower right*) a crawling amoeba magnified 300 times.

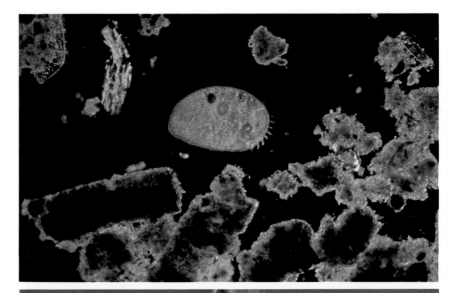

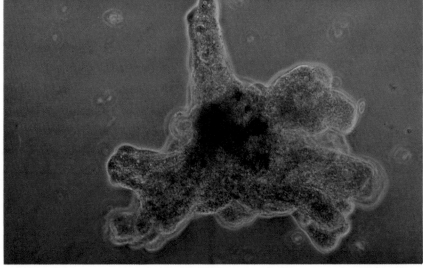

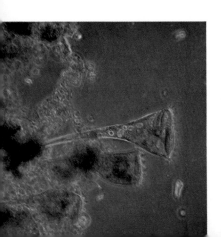

cell up to the full amount. But the DNA is a new mixture because it has come from not just one parent but two. So the fertilized egg may develop into an adult which is slightly different from either of its parents. When this first happened, it speeded up the rate at which organisms could evolve to become better suited to their surroundings.

There are about 10,000 species of protistans. Some are covered by threads, which beat together to drive the creature through the water. Others, including the amoeba, move by bulging out fingers from the main body and then flowing into them. Many of those that live in the sea make shells. Some feed by using chlorophyll and these can be called plants. The remainder of the group, which feed on them, can be labelled animals.

A few protistans are just large enough to see with the naked eye. With a little practice, you can pick out in a drop of pond water the speck of jelly which is an amoeba. But single-celled creatures cannot

Protistan shells
One group of protistans, the radiolarians, build themselves complicated shells of silica, the substance from which glass is made. These are the empty shells magnified 1500 times.

The endless variety

grow large for, as size increases, the chemical processes inside the cell work less well. Size, however, can be achieved in a different way – by grouping cells together in a colony.

One species that has done this is volvox, a hollow globe, almost the size of a pinhead, built from a large number of cells, each with a flagellum. These units are almost the same as other single cells that swim by themselves, but these are coordinated. All the flagella around the globe beat together and drive the tiny ball in a particular direction.

This kind of coordination between cells in a colony went a stage further, probably between 800 and 1000 million years ago – sometime in October in our calendar – when sponges appeared. A sponge can grow very big — 2 m or so across. But the bonds between its cells are very loose. Some cells crawl over the sponge like amoebae. If a sponge is forced through a sieve so that it is broken down into separate cells, these will eventually organize themselves back into a sponge. Sponges feed by filtering food particles from streams of water passing through tubes in their body. But they can hardly be counted as proper many-celled animals. They have no nerves and no muscles. The simplest creatures to possess such things as these are the jellyfish and their relatives.

Volvox colonies
Inside many of these hollow globes, there are daughter colonies. In time the parent colonies will split to release them.

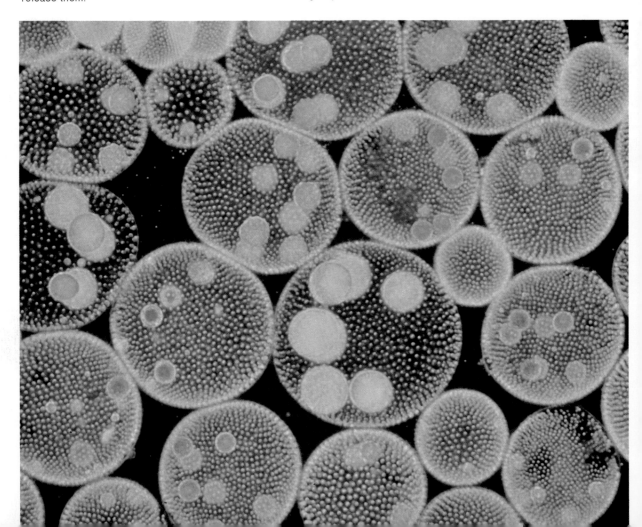

A group of sponges

An Indian Ocean sponge

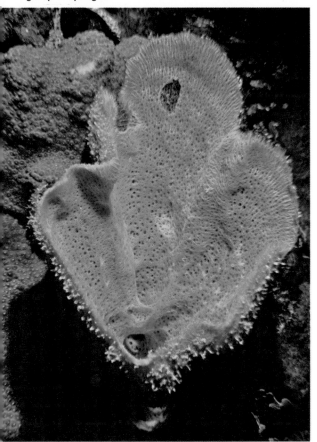

A Caribbean sponge

A candlestick sponge from the Red Sea

The endless variety

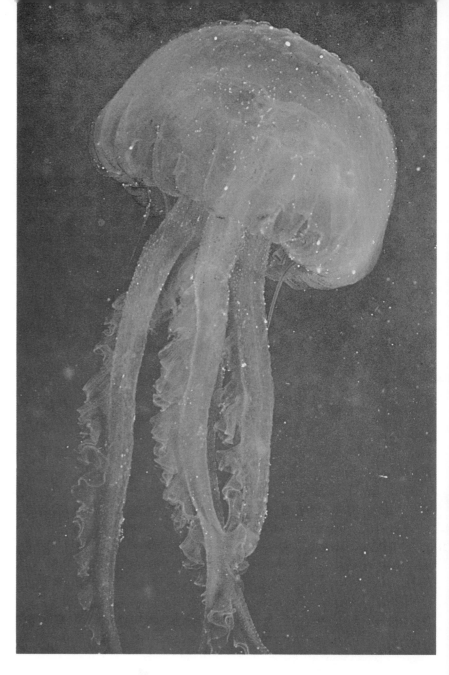

Jellyfish
This species of jellyfish (*right and below*) is luminous and shines at night like a glowing white ball. It sometimes occurs in densely-packed shoals of many thousands that may stretch for as much as 40 km.

A typical jellyfish is a saucer fringed with stinging tentacles. This form is called a medusa. It has two layers of cells separated by jelly which gives the creature enough firmness to withstand the rough sea. Their cells, unlike those of the sponge, cannot survive independently. Some are linked to form simple nerves. Others which are able to shorten themselves become simple muscles.

Jellyfish reproduce by releasing eggs and sperm into the sea which then meet and fuse together. But the fertilized egg becomes something quite different from its parents. It settles down at the bottom of the sea and grows into a tiny flower-like creature called a polyp. In some species, this sprouts other polyps. They filter-feed with the aid of tiny beating hairs. Eventually, the polyps sprout buds

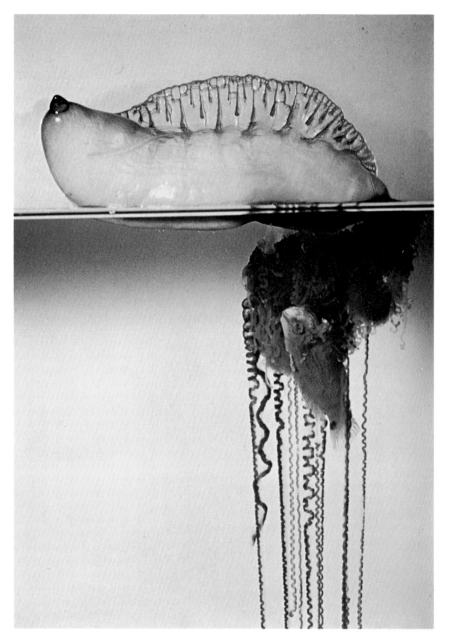

The Portuguese Man o' War
Some polyps have formed colonies
and taken to the floating life like
medusae. The Portuguese Man o'
War is one. The polyps hang down
in strings (*above*) from a gas-filled
float (*left*). Their stings are
extremely poisonous and paralyse
the fish on which the colony feeds.

A fire jellyfish
This small jellyfish (*below*) is
sometimes called a sea wasp for
the slightest touch of its tentacles
causes very painful burns. This one
has just caught a fish.

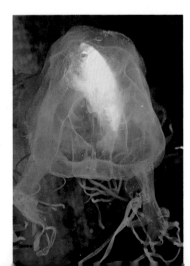

which break off and become miniature medusae. These wriggle
away and take up the swimming life once more.

The true jellyfish spend most of their time as free-floating medusae
with only a short period fixed to the rocks. Others, like the sea
anemones, do the reverse. For all their adult lives they are polyps,
glued to the rocks, their tentacles waving in the water ready to trap
prey that may touch them.

It is difficult to believe that such soft fragile creatures as jellyfish
could be fossilized, but in the 1940s, some shapes like jellyfish were
found in rocks in Australia that are about 650 million years old.
They are the marks left by jellyfish which were stranded on the beach,
baked in the sun and then covered with sand by the next tide.

The endless variety

Sea anemones

There are over a thousand different kinds of these creatures with many varied and beautiful colours. A few live on the deep ocean floor, but most like these (*right*) are found in shallower waters and in rock pools close to the shore. Their eggs, squirted into the water become, after fertilization, tiny medusae which are swept far and wide by ocean currents before settling down and growing into polyps. They have stings in their tentacles with which they catch small creatures such as fish and shrimps (*below*).

At least 16 different kinds of these fossil jellyfish have now been recognized. There are also fossils of colonial forms that lived fixed to the sea floor. These lie in the dusty brown sandstone like long feathers. Closely similar creatures called sea pens still live in the sea. They grow sticking up vertically on sandy sea floors, some only a few centimetres long, some half as tall as a human. At night they are particularly spectacular for they glow bright purple and if you touch them, ghostly waves of light move along their slowly writhing arms.

Sea pens are also called soft corals. Stony corals, their relatives, often grow alongside them and they too are colonial creatures. Their history is not as ancient as that of the sea pens but once they had appeared, they flourished in immense number.

Sea pens, ancient and modern
Fossil shapes (*below*) found in sandstones in southern Australia may be the remains of creatures like sea pens stranded on a sandy beach 650 million years ago. Living sea pens (*left*) still live in the tropical seas.

The endless variety

The first time you dive on a coral reef is a wonderful experience. There are domes, branches and fans, antlers tipped with blue, organ pipes that are blood red. But if you swim only during the day, you will hardly ever see the organisms that have created this astounding scene. At night, with a torch in your hand, you will find the coral transformed. The sharp outlines of the colonies now have haloes. Millions of tiny polyps have emerged from their limestone cells to stretch out their arms and grope for food.

Coral polyps are each only a few millimetres across, but working together in colonies they have produced the greatest animal construction in the world before humans began their labours. The Great Barrier Reef, running along the eastern coast of Australia for over 1500 km, can be seen from the moon. So if, some 500 million years ago, astronauts from some other planet had passed near the earth, they could easily have noticed in the blue seas, a few new and mysterious shapes of paler blue. From them they might have guessed that life on earth had really started.

The tiny island-builders
The coral polyps (*above*) build shells of limestone around themselves. Each species forms colonies by branching in a different way (*right*). Together they form thick reefs in tropical shallow water. Over centuries, the waves destroy the skeletons of the colonies, grinding them into sand and so buiding small coral islands.

2· Building bodies

The Great Barrier Reef swarms with life. Purple eyes peer out from beneath shells. Starfish of an intense blue spangle the sand. Dive down through the clear water and turn a boulder. A flat ribbon, striped yellow and scarlet, dances gracefully away and an emerald green brittle star rushes over the sand on writhing catherine-wheel arms to find a new hiding place.

The variety at first seems bewildering, but leaving aside simple creatures like jellyfish and corals which we have already looked at, and the much more advanced backboned fish, nearly all belong to one of three main types: shelled animals, like clams, cowries and sea snails; round creatures like starfish and sea urchins; and longer animals with jointed bodies varying from wriggling bristle worms to shrimps and lobsters. These creatures are all called invertebrates – animals without backbones.

These three kinds of bodies are so different that it seems unlikely that they are closely related to one another. The fossil record shows this is so. All three groups have left behind plenty of remains which can be traced back to rocks that were laid down 600 million years ago. In these, the shelled animals are represented by small shells called brachiopods; the round creatures by flower-like fossils called crinoids; and the animals with jointed bodies, by little creatures like woodlice called trilobites. But then, suddenly, there are no fossils at all. Rocks that are older than this are almost entirely without remains of animals except microscopic ones and there are none that show clearly how these groups might be related to one another. If we want to find out about that, we have to look elsewhere.

We can find some living clues back on the reef. Fluttering over the coral heads, hiding in the cracks or clinging to the underside of rocks, are flat leaf-shaped worms. Like jellyfish, they have only one

A flatworm

Underwater on the Great Barrier Reef (*left*)

Flatworms
These simple creatures crawl over rocks and coral (*above and below*), but they can also swim through open water (*top*) by rippling their bodies.

opening to their gut through which they pass both food and water. They have no gills and breathe directly through their skin. Their front end has a mouth below and a few light-sensitive spots above so that the animals can be said to have the beginnings of a head. The flatworm is the simplest creature to show signs of such a thing.

To be of any use, eyespots must be linked to muscles so that the animal can react to what it senses. In flatworms all that exists is a simple network of nerve fibres. Yet the flatworms have surprising powers. One freshwater type, for example, can learn. They have been trained to find their way through a simple maze, choosing white passages and avoiding dark ones by being given slight electric shocks when they made a wrong decision. Even more surprisingly, that memory has been shown to stay in their bodies. If a worm that has learned the maze is eaten by another worm, the new one will run the maze correctly without training.

Today there are some 3000 species of flatworm in the world. Most are tiny and water-living. Others live on land in humid tropical forests. Some flatworms, such as liverflukes and tapeworms, are parasites and live within the bodies of other animals, including humans.

Flatworms are very simple creatures. One group of them look very like the tiny free-swimming creatures that later in their lives settle down to become corals. So it seems likely that the flatworms are descended from simpler creatures like corals and jellyfish.

In the period when these first sea invertebrates were developing, between 600 and 1000 million years ago, erosion or weathering produced a lot of mud and sand on the sea bed. This offered protection for any creature that lived within it. But the flatworm shape is not suited to burrowing. A tube-like form is much more useful and eventually worms with such a shape appeared. Some became active burrowers, tunnelling through the mud in search of

food. Others lived half-buried with their mouths above the mud, filtering their food from the water.

Some of these creatures lived in a protective tube. In time, others developed two flat, protective shells. These were the first brachiopods. One of them, named Lingulella, gave rise to a line of descendants that still live today, almost unchanged. They are what have been called living fossils.

They look like long worms with two small horny shells at one end. The body, however, is quite complicated. It has a digestive tube that ends in an anus, or opening for discarding waste, and a group of tentacles around the mouth, enclosed within the two shells. Food particles in the water are caught by the tentacles and passed by them down to the mouth. The tentacles serve another important purpose for the water brings with it dissolved oxygen. The tentacles absorb the oxygen and so serve as gills.

The brachiopods changed over the next 100 million years or so. Many species developed a hole in the shell through which a stalk fastened the animal into the mud. This gave the shell the look of an upside-down Roman oil lamp, with the stalk as the wick, which is why they are called lamp-shells.

The brachiopods are not the only shelled worms whose fossils are found in these ancient rocks. Another kind developed in which the worm did not attach itself to the sea floor. It made a shell to protect itself as it crawled about. This was the ancestor of the most successful group of all shelled worms, the molluscs. Today there are about 60,000 different species of molluscs.

The lower part of the mollusc's body is called the foot. The animal moves by sticking out its foot from the shell and rippling the undersurface. Some molluscs have a small disc of shell attached to the foot which closes the entrance when the animal withdraws into the shell. The upper surface of the body is formed by a thin sheet that

A mollusc: the top shell

Building bodies

covers the internal organs and is called the mantle. In a hollow between it and the central part of the body, most species have gills.

The shell is produced by the surface of the mantle. Some molluscs have just one shell. They feed not with tentacles within the shell like the brachiopods but with a rough tongue. Some scrape algae from the rock with it. Whelks carry it on a stalk and use it to bore holes into other molluscs and kill them. The tongue of cone shells has become a kind of gun. From the end of it they shoot a tiny harpoon. While the victim – a worm or even a fish – struggles, they inject a poison so strong that it kills the prey instantly. It can even be deadly to a human. They then haul the prey back to the shell and slowly engulf it.

For hunting, a heavy shell is a handicap. Some carnivorous molluscs have taken to a faster if riskier life by doing without it altogether like their flatworm-like ancestors. These are the sea slugs. Their long soft bodies are covered on the upper side with waving tentacles of the most delicate colours and patterns. Though they lack shells, they are not entirely defenceless, for some have acquired secondhand weapons. These species float near the surface of the water on feathery tentacles and hunt jellyfish. As the sea slug eats its prey, the stinging cells of the victim are taken into its gut, and are stored in the tentacles on its back. There they protect the sea slug just as they did the original jellyfish.

A cone shell on the attack
It has stuck out its tongue and shot a barb from the end of it into the huge foot of another mollusc.

Sea slugs
These molluscs without shells (*below*) are only a few centimetres long. Glaucus (*right*) has developed tentacles that enable it to float on the surface of the sea and feed on jellyfish.

Life in the sea 530 million years ago

Some of the most perfectly preserved fossils in the world have been found in mudstones that form one cliff in the Rocky Mountains of Canada. Even the remains of small soft-bodied creatures have been discovered here. Together they have made it possible to put together a detailed picture of the sea bed at this very early period when animals were first beginning to swarm in the seas.

Sea lilies grow on the sea floor like strange plants. Flatworms and jellyfish, shaped like pineapple rings, drift through the waters. In the background on the right a mollusc with spines on its back ploughs its way through the mud towards a group of sponges.

A large trilobite crawls over the rocks in the left foreground, feeling its way with a pair of long curling antennae and a shoal of smaller trilobites swims in the lower right-hand corner. Many other segmented creatures existed at this time. A large one is swimming above the big trilobite and two smaller ones are groping with their pincers beneath it. Some of these creatures were very strange indeed and quite unlike anything alive today. The big animal near the bottom in the middle is such a creature. It had five eyes and a single long grasping tentacle.

Bivalves: molluscs with two-part shells

The scallop (*above*) is about 10 cm long and has a line of simple eyes along the edge of its mantle. Both the scallop and the file shell (*bottom*) can escape from enemies by clapping the halves of their shells together and so leaping through the water. The biggest mollusc of all is the giant clam (*right*) which grows to well over 1 m across. It is so big that it cannot move and coral usually grows up around it so that all that can be seen is the edge of its shell with the green mantle between the two halves.

Other molluscs, like mussels and clams, have shells divided into two parts, or valves. They are called bivalves. For the most part, they feed by filtering food from the water, sucking water in through one end of the space below the mantle and squirting it out at the other. Since they do not need to move, they can grow to a great size. Giant clams on the reef may grow to be 1 m long. Some filter-feeders like the scallops do manage to travel by clapping their shells together and so make curving leaps. But most bivalves live a fixed life.

One branch of the molluscs found a way of becoming highly mobile and yet keeping the protection of a large and heavy shell – they developed gas-filled flotation tanks. The first such creature appeared about 550 million years ago. Its flat-coiled shell was not completely filled with flesh as is that of a snail, but had a hind end

walled off to form a gas chamber. As the animal grew, new chambers were added to balance the increasing weight. This creature was the nautilus and one member of its family, the pearly nautilus, still survives. It grows to about 20 cm across. A tube runs from the back of the body chamber into the flotation tanks at the rear so that the animal can flood them and float at whatever level it wishes. The nautilus feeds not only on dead animals or carrion, but on living creatures such as crabs. It moves by jet propulsion, squirting water through a siphon. It searches for its prey with the help of small stalked eyes and tentacles. Its foot has become divided into 90 or so long grasping tentacles with which it grapples with its prey. In the centre of them it has a horny beak, which can deliver a shell-cracking bite.

The pearly nautilus
The two (*above*) are feeding on a lobster. The nautilus shell, when cut in half (*below*), shows the flotation chambers which, in life, are filled with gas.

Fossil ammonites

The many shapes of a hunting octopus

After some 140 million years of development, the nautilus gave rise to another group with many more flotation chambers to each shell, the ammonites. These animals thrived. In some rocks their fossilized shells lie so thickly that they form solid bands. Some ammonites grew as big as lorry wheels but they were nearly weightless in water. Some types may even have sailed like galleons across the surface of the prehistoric oceans.

About 100 million years ago, for reasons that we do not understand, the ammonite dynasty began to die out. Eventually all the shelled forms except the pearly nautilus disappeared. But the shell-less ones survived. They became the most intelligent of all the molluscs, the squid and octopus.

Traces of the squid's ancestral shell can be found deep within it as a horny blade. The octopus, however, has lost all traces of

its shell. The squid has many fewer tentacles than the nautilus – only ten – and the octopus, however, as its name makes clear, has only eight. Of the two creatures, the squids are much the more mobile and have fins running along their sides which help propel the animal through the water. Both creatures can use jet propulsion like the nautilus.

Squids grow to an immense size. In 1954 one was washed ashore in Norway that measured 9 m from the end of its body to the tip of its outstretched tentacles and weighed about a tonne. Even this was not the largest. In 1933, in New Zealand, one was recorded that was 21 m long with eyes 40 cm across, the largest known eyes in the whole animal kingdom. Even now we are unlikely to have discovered the biggest that exists. They are the most surprising descendants of the simple little shells that first appeared 600 million years ago.

Cuttlefish and squid
(*Above*) cuttlefish are related to squid. The relic of their shells is cuttlebone. (*Below*) a squid.

Building bodies

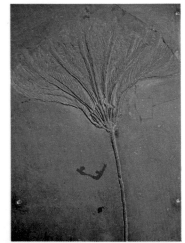

Crinoids
(*Top*) a fossil sea lily from a limestone about 70 million years old; (*above*) living sea lilies from the deep sea; (*right*) a living featherstar – a creature that resembles a sea lily but has no stem.

A sea urchin from the Barrier Reef

But what of the second great category, the one represented in ancient rocks by the flower-like crinoids? Each crinoid has a central body rising from a stem like the seedhead of a poppy. From this sprout five arms which, in some species, branch repeatedly. The surface is made up of closely-fitting lime plates. These creatures, like the ammonites, have had their day, but a few species, known as sea lilies, still survive in the ocean depths.

The lime plates are embedded just under the skin. This gives their surface a curious prickly feel. In related families, the skin has spines and needles attached to it so the creatures are known as echinoderms, or 'spiny skins'. The basic pattern on which the echinoderm body is built has five elements. The lime plates are five-sided; there are five arms; and all the internal organs are in groups of five.

The five-sided body is such a distinctive characteristic that it makes members of the group very easy to recognize. The starfish and their more sprightly cousins, the brittle stars, both show it. These creatures appear to be crinoids that have no stalk and are lying upside-down with their mouths on the ground and their five arms outstretched. Sea urchins are obviously related. They seem to have curled their arms up from the mouth as five ribs and then connected them by more plates to form a globe.

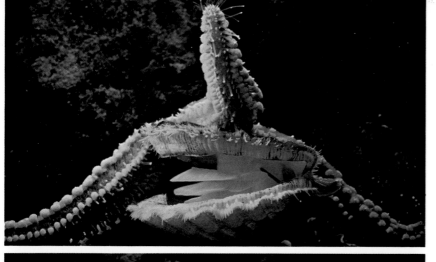

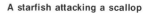

A starfish attacking a scallop

Starfish
A blue starfish (*far left*) and a rhinoceros starfish (*near left*) are both common on the Great Barrier Reef. A brittle star (*bottom far left*) with five writhing arms and a sun star (*bottom near left*), like all echinoderms, move with the help of tube feet (*below*).

Sea cucumbers
(*Top*) the feathery tentacles around the mouth of this kind of sea cucumber catch particles of food from the water. (*Above*) a disturbed sea cucumber throws out its internal organs.

Segmented animals
(*Right*) a fossil trilobite about 400 million years old. It is about 5 cm long. (*Below*) a segmented worm lying in its tube in the sand.

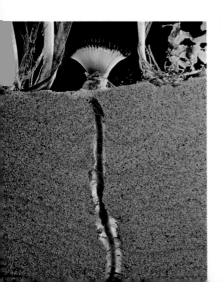

The sausage-like sea cucumbers that sprawl on sandy patches in the reef are also echinoderms which lie on their sides. At one end is an opening used for breathing and disposing waste. The mouth at the other end is surrounded by tube feet that have become enlarged into short tentacles for feeding. If you pick up a sea cucumber, do so with care, for they have an amazing way of defending themselves. They simply press out their internal organs. A flood of sticky material pours out of the opening, fastening your fingers together. When a fish or crab provokes them to such action, it finds itself struggling in a mesh of threads while the sea cucumber slowly inches itself away. Over the next few weeks it will slowly grow itself a new set of internal organs.

The third category of creatures on the reef contains those with jointed or segmented bodies. In this instance, we do have fossil evidence of even earlier forms than the trilobites that accompany those early ancestors of the other two groups. These are prints of segmented worms that have been found beside the fossil jellyfish of Australia. Segmentation probably developed as a way of helping worms to burrow in mud. A line of separate limbs down each side is very useful for this purpose and it could have been acquired by repeating the simple body unit to form a chain. After these early worms, the history of segmented creatures remains invisible for 100 million years. Only after this vast span do we reach the period, 600 million years ago, when there were trilobites.

The body armour of trilobites was made partly of lime and partly of a horny material. But it was not expandable and as the creature

grew, it had to shed its shell regularly. Many trilobite fossils are these empty suits of armour. A few, however, are of trilobites that were buried in mud before their bodies decayed. In the most perfectly preserved we can see paired jointed legs that are attached to each body segment, a feathery gill on a stalk alongside each leg, two feelers at the front of the head, a gut running the entire length of the body, even the muscles along the back which enabled the animal to roll itself up into a ball. Trilobites were the first creatures we know of that developed compound eyes. Each eye was a mosaic, a cluster of as many as 15,000 separate lenses, that enabled its owner to see an entire half circle.

As the trilobites spread through the seas of the world, many different kinds developed. Most seem to have lived on the sea floor. Some colonized the deep seas, where there was little light and lost their eyes altogether. Others may have paddled about, legs up-permost, scanning the sea floor below with their large eyes. In due course, as creatures of many other kinds came to live on the bottom of the seas, the trilobites lost their supremacy. 250 million years ago their rule ended. One distant relation alone survives, the horseshoe crab. Measuring 30 cm or so across, it is many times bigger than the largest known trilobite and its armour no longer shows any sign of segmentation. Instead, it forms a large shield on the front of which are two compound eyes. A rectangular plate, hinged to the back of the shield, carries a spiky tail. But beneath its shell, the segmentation is clear. It has several pairs of jointed legs with pincers on the end and behind these, gills which are large and flat like the leaves of a book.

Horseshoe crabs
Every year they come up out of the sea to spawn in the sand of the beach.

Although the trilobites were so successful, they were by no means the only armoured creatures to develop from the segmented worms. Another group, the crustaceans, appeared at about the same time. They survived the millions of years of trilobite rule and, when trilobites died out, it was they who took over. Today there are about 35,000 species of crustaceans – four times as many as there are of birds. Most prowl among the rocks and reefs – crabs, shrimps, prawns and lobsters. Some do not move at all – the barnacles; others swim in vast shoals – the krill which forms the food of whales. The shell acts as a skeleton which supports the animal's body not from the inside, as ours does, but from the outside. This external skeleton has been adapted to suit the tiny water flea as well as the giant Japanese spider crab that measures over 3 m from claw to claw.

Some crustaceans
(*Above*) krill, a shrimp that swims in huge swarms near the surface of the sea; (*right*) a rock crab; (*bottom*) hermit crabs. The back part of the hermit crab's body is soft (*left*) and normally it tucks this inside the empty shell of a mollusc (*right*).

Each species of crustacean adapts the shape of its many paired legs for particular purposes. Those at the front may become pincers or claws; those in the middle, paddles, walking legs or tweezers. Others develop attachments so that they can carry eggs. The limbs, which are tube-like and jointed, are moved by muscles that run down inside them.

The external skeleton gives the crustaceans the same problem it gave the trilobites. It will not expand and since it completely encloses their bodies, the only way they can grow is to shed it periodically. As the time for the shedding, or moult, approaches the animal absorbs many of the minerals from its shell into its blood. It grows a new, soft wrinkled skin beneath the shell. The outgrown armour splits and the animal pulls itself out, leaving its skeleton looking like a ghost of its

A moulting prawn
The prawn has just climbed out of its old shell which lies, empty, beneath it.

A spiny lobster

Building bodies

A land crab
Its claws are spread to defend itself.

A fiddler crab
The males use their single big claws to signal to one another.

former self. Now its skin is soft and it must hide. But it grows fast, stretching out the wrinkles of its new shell. Gradually this hardens and the animal can safely go out into the world.

The external skeleton has one quality which has had momentous results. Mechanically, it works almost as well on land as it does in water. There is nothing to prevent a creature with one walking straight out of the sea and up the beach if it can find a way of breathing there. Many crustaceans have done so. Sand shrimps and beach hoppers stay quite close to the sea. Woodlice have colonized moist ground throughout the land.

The most spectacular of all these land-living crustaceans is the robber crab. It is so big that it can grasp the trunk of a palm tree between its front legs. It climbs the palm with ease and cuts down the young coconuts on which it feeds with its gigantic pincers. At the back of its main shell there is an opening to an air chamber through which the crab absorbs oxygen. It returns to the sea to lay its eggs, but otherwise it is entirely at home on land.

Other descendants of the marine invertebrates have also left the water. Among the molluscs, there are the snails and the shell-less slugs. But the first to make the move to land were descendants of the segmented worms. Some 400 million years ago they found ways of surviving out of water and they made such a success of life on land that they in the end gave rise to the most numerous and varied of all land animals, the insects.

A robber crab climbing a tree

3 · The first forests

There are few more barren places on earth than the plains surrounding a volcano after an eruption. Black tides of lava lie spilt over its sides like slag from a furnace. Steam hisses between the blocks of lava. Pools of liquid mud, grey, yellow or blue, boil and bubble, heated by the hot lava far below. Otherwise all is still. No bush grows to give shelter from the wind. No speck of green relieves the black surface of the empty ash plains.

For the greater part of its history the earth's landscape was desolate like this. Long after life in the sea developed into many forms, the land remained lifeless. Some marine algae must have managed to live on the edges of the seas, rimming the beaches with green, but they could not have spread far beyond the water for they would have dried out and died. Then about 420 million years ago, some forms developed a waxy covering to stop them drying out. Even so, they could not leave the water because their reproductive processes depended on it.

Algae reproduce themselves in two ways – simply by dividing in half and by the sexual method in which male and female cells meet each other and join in pairs. In order to come together, they need water. Primitive land plants living today, such as liverworts and mosses, still reproduce sexually in this way. Plants like liverworts and mosses were probably among the earliest forms to colonize the moist edges of the land, but so far no fossilized mosses have been discovered from this early period. The first land plants we know, dating from over 400 million years ago, are simple leafless branching strands. Like moss, they had no roots, but their stems contained tubes for carrying water up the stem. These gave them strength and enabled them to stand several centimetres tall. That may not sound very impressive, but it was a major development.

Such plants, together with primitive mosses and liverworts, formed miniature forests that spread inland from the water and into these the first animal colonists crept from the sea. They were segmented creatures, ancestors of today's millipedes. At first they doubtless kept close to the edge of the water, but wherever there was moss there was both moisture and vegetable waste to eat. With the

A field of recently erupted lava
Reunion Island in the Indian Ocean.

Primitive land plants
(*Left*) a liverwort sprouting its reproductive capsules; (*middle*) the reproductive capsules of a moss; (*right*) a cushion of mosses.

Primitive land animals
(*Right*) a moulting centipede crawling out of its old skin; (*below*) millipedes mating; (*bottom*) a giant millipede, central America.

land to themselves, these pioneering creatures thrived. Their name millipede, 'thousand legs', is an exaggeration. No species alive today has many more than 200 legs and some have as few as eight. Nevertheless, the first ones grew to magnificent sizes. One of them was 2 m long and must have had a devastating effect on the plants as it browsed its way through the wet green bogs. It was, after all, as long as a cow.

The external skeleton inherited from their water-living ancestors enabled them to move about on land, but the millipedes did have to develop a different way of breathing. The gills used by the crustaceans in water would not work in air. In their place, the millipedes developed a system of breathing tubes which open on their sides and branch internally into a fine network which takes oxygen to all parts of the body.

Reproduction out of water also posed problems for the millipedes. Their marine ancestors had relied on water to carry the sperm to the eggs. On land the solution was an obvious one – male and female must meet and pass the sperm directly from one to the other. This is exactly what millipedes do. Both sexes produce their reproductive cells from glands close to the base of the second pair of legs. When the male meets the female in the mating season, the two intertwine. The male reaches forward with his seventh leg, collects a bundle of sperm from his sex gland and then clambers alongside the female and holds the bundle alongside her sexual pouch so that she can take it in. The process looks rather clumsy but at least it is not dangerous. Millipedes are entirely vegetarian. So there is no risk that, when they come together to mate, they might eat one another.

But some of the early land invertebrates were hunters. Three groups of them still survive today – centipedes, scorpions and spiders. Like their prey, they are segmented animals, but in varying degrees. The centipedes are as clearly segmented as the millipedes. The scorpions show divisions only in their long tails and most (though not all) spiders have lost all signs of segmentation.

The scorpions resemble creatures, now long extinct, called sea scorpions that at this period terrorized the oceans. Some grew to a length of 2 m and were armed with immense pincers with which they seized smaller creatures. The land scorpions were distant relatives and certainly shared the same savage habits.

The scorpions that live today have not only fearsome-looking claws but a large poison gland with a sting drooping from the end of the tail. Because they are so dangerous their mating cannot be the somewhat hit-and-miss gropings practised by the millipedes. The mate runs the risk of being regarded not as a mate but a meal. So scorpion mating demands, for the first time among the animals that have appeared so far in this history, the rituals of courtship.

The male scorpion approaches the female with great care. Suddenly he grabs her pincers with his. Thus linked, with her

The stinging tail of a scorpion

The scorpions' mating dance

A scorpion mother
Her young are clinging to her back.

A scorpion eating a grasshopper

weapons neutralized, the pair begin to dance. Backwards and forwards they move with their tails held upright, sometimes even intertwined. The male then produces a packet of sperm from his sexual opening and deposits it on the ground. Still grasping the female by the claws, he jerks and heaves her forward until her sexual opening, also on her underside, is directly above the sperm packet. She takes it up and the partners separate. The eggs eventually hatch inside the mother's pouch, the young crawl out and clamber up onto her back. There they stay for about a fortnight until they have completed their first moult and can fend for themselves.

Spiders, too, must be extremely cautious in their courtship. It is even more dangerous for the male because he is nearly always smaller than the female. He prepares for his encounter with his mate long before he meets her. He spins a tiny triangle of silk and deposits a drop of sperm onto it from the gland that lies underneath his body. He then sucks it into the hollow first joint of a special limb. Now he is ready.

Jumping spiders and wolf spiders hunt primarily by sight and have excellent eyes. So the courting male relies on visual signals to make the female aware of him. His front limbs are brightly coloured and patterned and he waves them at the female. Spiders that are active at night depend largely on touch to find their prey. So when the male and female meet, they reassure one another with caresses. In web-making species the male signals to a female by twanging the threads at one side of the web in a special way which he trusts she will recognize. Other species put their faith in bribery. The male catches an insect and parcels it up in silk. Holding this in front of him, he cautiously approaches the female and presents it to her. While she is occupied in examining the gift, he quickly ties her to the ground with bonds of silk before he risks an embrace.

Wolf spiders courting
The male on the right is signalling to the female by waving his front limbs.

The savage spiders
The female green orb spider (*left*) catches her prey with a web and will eat most things that venture onto it. A male must do so during mating and often is eaten by her afterwards as is shown here. The baboon spider (*below*) hunts on the ground. The crab spider (*bottom*) has huge jaws and often lurks on flowers awaiting its victims.

All these techniques lead to the same conclusion. The male thrusts his special limb into the female's sexual opening, squirts out the sperm and then hastily retreats. In spite of all his precautions, he sometimes fails to make his getaway in time and the female eats him after all. But in terms of the success of the species as a whole, that individual disaster is unimportant. He had completed his purpose before he lost his life.

The plants and animals that colonized the land

This painting shows a scene some 380 million years ago when life was first beginning to spread from water onto the land. The fossils on which it is based come from many different parts of the world.

The very first land plants grew on the moist edges of lakes and creeks and were only

about 5 cm in height. Later, others developed that resembled the clubmosses of today. One is shown here on the left of the picture. It is sprouting capsules full of spores. Within the stems of these plants ran tubes with thick walls that carried the sap to and from the thorn-like leaves. Even with such stout tubes

inside them, the stems were not very rigid and none of these plants grew to more than 1 or 2 m tall. They did, however, represent food for plant-eating animals and eventually such creatures emerged from the water and browsed in these miniature jungles. Other creatures then appeared that preyed on the vegetarians. In the foreground of this picture one of these hunters, a scorpion with its stinging tail arched above it, is battling with a centipede. On the stem of the giant clubmoss behind them lurks an early spider-like creature. In the bottom left-hand corner, an early wingless insect is munching vegetation.

The first forests

Ferns
Some kinds develop trunks and grow very tall like the tree ferns in the rain forests of southern Australia (*right*). All of them produce reproductive cells from small organs which grow beneath the leaves (*below*). They vary in shape according to the species.

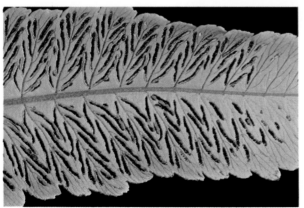

While the early segmented animals were adapting to living on land, the plants were also changing. Neither the mosses nor the other early forms had true roots, which meant they could only live in moist surroundings. But where the only permanent water supply lay below the ground, plants needed roots to bring up water from the soil. Three groups of plants eventually appeared with roots – club-mosses, horsetails and ferns. All three had strong woody tubes within their stems to carry the water absorbed by their roots. This inner strength also enabled them to grow tall. All green plants depend on light to feed and grow. If they are overshadowed by another, they may die from lack of light. So these early plant groups used the strength of their stems to grow very tall. They became trees.

A horsetail

The height of these first forests must have caused problems for the animals. Once, there had been plenty of leaves close to the ground. Now the soaring trunks had raised this source of food high in the sky. So many of the vegetarian animals had to clamber up the trunks to find food. Perhaps they also left the ground to escape from the first backboned creatures that were now appearing on land – the amphibians for they were meat-eaters.

Some of these land invertebrate families still survive. They are the bristletails and springtails. Although they are rarely seen, they are enormously plentiful. There is hardly a spadeful of soil anywhere in the world that does not contain some of them but only one is commonly noticed, the silverfish that glides across cellar floors. Its body is segmented but it has very many fewer parts than the millipede. It has a head with compound eyes and antennae; a thorax, or middle section, bearing three pairs of legs; and a segmented abdomen which, while it no longer has legs on each segment, has little stumps as signs that it once had them. Three thin threads trail from its tail. It breathes like the millipedes by means of internal tubes and it reproduces in a way similar to those early land invertebrates, the scorpions.

Clubmoss

There are several thousand different species within this group. They all have six legs and the same three parts to their bodies. This makes them members of that great and varied group of land invertebrates, the insects.

A silverfish
This creature, a direct descendant of the early plant-eating land animals, prefers cool damp places and is often found today in cellars.

The first forces

Early insect flyers
The first known flying insects had two pairs of independently operating wings as does the damselfly (*right*) and the dragonfly (*below*) today.

A cicada
In flight, the back edge of this insect's front wing fits into a groove or is hooked onto the front edge of the hind wing to form a single surface.

The primitive insects must have found some of their food by climbing the trunks of the early tree ferns and horsetails. But others developed a swifter way of getting from tree to tree. They flew.

The earliest insects with wings that we know are the dragonflies. They appeared some 300 million years ago. Most were about the size of those living today but some grew to an enormous size, with a wingspan of 70 cm, the largest insects ever to exist.

Dragonflies have two pairs of wings which have simple joints to them. They can only move up and down and cannot be folded back. Even so, they are skilful flyers, shooting over the surface of a pond at up to 30 km/h. At such speeds, they need accurate sense organs if they are to avoid collisions. They navigate with the help of huge mosaic eyes on either side of the head which provide superb vision. Because of this dependence on sight, the dragonflies cannot be active at night. They are daytime hunters, flying with their six legs crooked in front of them to form a tiny basket in which they catch smaller insects.

Dragonflies beat their front wings and back wings at the same time. Their wings do not normally touch, but even so there are problems when the dragonfly makes sharp turns. Then the fore- and hind wings, bending under the stress of turning, beat against one another making a rattle that you can easily hear.

Flies
The flies use only their front wings for flying. The rear pair have become small twirling drumsticks that help in balancing and navigation. They are difficult to see in the blowfly (*left*) but large and obvious in the crane fly (*above*).

An ancient fly
This fly got trapped in the resin oozing from the trunk of a conifer tree about 50 million years ago. The resin became fossilized as amber, preserving the fly within it.

The later insect groups seem to have found that it is better to fly with just one pair of wing surfaces. Bees and wasps hitch their fore- and hind wings together with hooks to make a single surface. Butterfly wings overlap. Hawkmoths, which are among the swiftest insect flyers capable of speeds of 50 km/h, have small hind wings which latch onto the long narrow forewings with a curved bristle. Beetles use only their back wings for flying. Their forewings have become very thick and act as covers to protect the delicate flying wings when they clamber about on the ground as most do.

The most accomplished aeronauts of all are the flies. They can fly at high speeds. Some can hover motionless in mid-air and even fly backwards. They use only their forewings for flight. The hind wings are reduced to thin stalks with tiny knobs at the end. When the fly is in the air, these move up and down a hundred or more times a second and help in balancing.

A slow flyer
The two pairs of a butterfly's wings overlap and so they beat together.

The insects were the first creatures to colonize the air and for 100 million years it was theirs alone. But their lives were not without danger. Their old enemies, the spiders, never developed wings, but they did not allow their insect prey to escape totally. They set traps of silk across the flyways between the branches and so continued to catch insects.

The flowers of the pine
The female flower of the pine appears first on the tip of the branch as a small red tuft. If it is fertilized, it becomes, after a year, a cone. The following year, the cone opens and the seeds fall out.

The advertising flowers
Magnolias (*below*) were among the first plants to bear true flowers. Their bright colours signalled the presence of pollen and so attracted insects. A honeybee (*right*) visits a crocus and will carry pollen away with it and so may fertilize the next crocus flower it lands on.

Plants now began to turn the flying skills of the insects to their own advantage. The early tree ferns had relied on the wind to distribute their reproductive cells. Now more advanced plants appeared with thick woody trunks. These carried their female cells in cones. Such conifers, which today include pine trees, still depend on the wind to carry the male cells, or pollen, to the female cones. But this is very wasteful, for the tree must produce vast quantities of pollen to make sure that all female flowers are fertilized with a grain. Most of it goes to waste.

Insects offered a much more efficient transport system. If properly encouraged, they could carry the small amount of pollen necessary for fertilization and place it on the exact spot in the female flower where it was needed. This messenger service would work best if both pollen and egg were placed close together on the plant so that the insects could make both deliveries and collections in the same call. And so developed the flower.

The simplest flowers are like the magnolia. They appeared about 100 million years ago. The eggs are clustered in the centre, each protected by a green coat with a spike on the top called a stigma (the female part of the flower). The pollen must be placed on the stigma if the eggs are to be fertilized. Grouped around the eggs are many stamens (the male part of the flower) producing pollen. The centre of the flower is surrounded by bright petals to attract insects.

Beetles had fed on the pollen of tree ferns and conifers and they were among the first to visit the early flowers like those of magnolias and waterlilies. As they moved from one to another, they collected

meals of pollen and paid for them by becoming covered in pollen which they accidentally delivered to the next flower they visited.

One danger of having both eggs and pollen in the same flower is that the plant may pollinate itself and so prevent cross-fertilization. This possibility is avoided in the magnolia, as in many plants, by having eggs and pollen that develop at different times.

The appearance of the flowers transformed the face of the world. The green forest now flared with colour as the plants advertised the rewards they had on offer. The first flowers were open to all and no particular skill was needed to gather their pollen. Such blooms attracted several kinds of insects – bees as well as beetles. But a variety of visitors has its disadvantages for they are also likely to call upon several kinds of flowers. Pollen of one species deposited in flowers of another is pollen wasted. So particular flowers and particular insects have tended to develop together, each adapting to the other's needs.

Right from the times of the giant horsetails and ferns, insects had been used to visiting the tops of trees to gather spores as food. Pollen was an almost identical diet and it still remains a most important prize. Bees collect it in great baskets on their thighs and take it back to their hives for eating or for turning into pollen bread for their young. Some plants produce two kinds of pollen – one that fertilizes their flowers and another particularly tasty kind that is meant only to be eaten. Other flowers developed a completely new bribe, nectar. The only purpose of this sweet liquid is to attract insects to the flower. With this the flowers recruited a whole new regiment of messengers, particularly bees, flies and butterflies.

An insect messenger
A honeybee carries pollen back to the hive in baskets on its hind legs (*left*). As it crawls around a flower (*top and bottom*), it accidentally becomes covered in pollen. It also sips nectar with its long tongue (*above*) which it will give up when it gets back to the hive so that it can be stored as honey to keep the colony fed over winter.

The signals of flowers
The mallow (*above*) and the yellow flag (*above right*) carry lines which point to where their pollen can be found. The fly orchid (*below*) attracts solitary wasps in a different way. It imitates a female wasp.

These prizes of pollen and nectar have to be advertised. The bright colours of flowers make them noticeable from far away. Markings on the petals show the insect the exact position of the rewards they seek. Some flowers are a different colour in the centre – forget-me-nots, hollyhocks, bindweed. Others are marked with lines and spots like an airfield to show the insect where to land and in which direction to taxi – foxgloves, violets, rhododendrons. There are more of these signals than we may realize. Many insects can see colours such as ultraviolet that are invisible to us. If we photograph what seem to be plain flowers with film that is sensitive to ultraviolet light, we can often discover markings on the petals that are used by insects.

Scent is also a major lure. In most cases, the perfumes that insects find attractive, such as those of lavender, roses, and honeysuckle, please us as well. But this is not always the case. For example, some plants smell like rotting meat in order to attract flies.

Perhaps the most bizarre imitations of all are those of some orchids that attract insects by impersonation. One produces a flower that looks like a female wasp complete with eyes, antennae and wings and even gives off the smell of a female wasp ready to mate. Male wasps are fooled and try to mate with it. As they do so, they deposit a load of pollen within the orchid flower and pick up a fresh batch to carry to the next false female.

The secret signs

The dots on a foxglove (*above*) and the lines on a pansy (*below left*) show clearly where an insect should go for pollen. Bees cannot see red. They can, however, see ultraviolet, a colour invisible to us. So the poppy (*left*) will appear to them as a white flower with black on the centre. The evening primrose (*below*) appears to us to have unmarked petals, but film sensitive to ultraviolet light reveals (*bottom*) that it too has landing signals visible to an insect.

The first forests

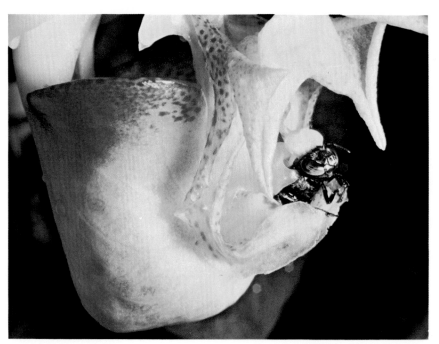

A bee in a bucket orchid (*right*)

The yucca and its moth
A yucca moth fertilizes the yucca plant by ramming a ball of pollen on the stigma of the flower (*below*). But it also lays its egg in the yucca's ovary (*bottom*) so that its grub will feed on some of the yucca's seeds, when they develop.

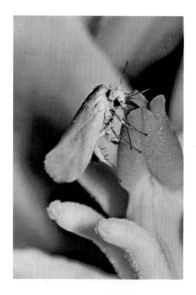

Sometimes insects do not collect pollen, preferring nectar. Then the flowers have to have ways to force their pollen on the insect. Some blooms have become obstacle courses during which their visitors are covered with pollen before they are able to leave. The bucket orchid from central America drugs its visitors. Bees clamber into its throat and sip a nectar so intoxicating that they begin to stagger about. The surface of the flower is slippery. The bees lose their foothold and are shot into a small bucket of liquid. The only way out of this is up a spout. As the drunken insect totters up, it has to wriggle beneath an overhanging rod which showers it with pollen.

Sometimes plant and insect become totally dependent one upon the other. The yucca grows in central America. It has a rosette of huge leaves from the centre of which rises a tall stalk bearing cream-coloured flowers. These attract a small moth with specially curved mouth parts that enable it to gather pollen from the yucca stamens. It moulds the pollen into a ball and then carries it off to another yucca flower. First it goes to the bottom of the flower and lays its eggs inside the ovary. Then it climbs back up to the top of the stigma rising from the ovary and rams the pollen ball into the top. The plant has now been fertilized and, in due course, the ovary will swell into seeds. The moth's eggs will hatch into caterpillars which feed on some of the seeds. The rest will develop into new yucca plants. If the moth were to become extinct, the yuccas would not reproduce themselves. Each depends on the other.

Flowers bloomed long before humans appeared on the earth. They developed in order to appeal to insects. Had butterflies been colour-blind and bees without a delicate sense of smell, we would have been denied some of the greatest delights that the natural world has to offer.

4 · Insect armies

The insect body is the most successful of all the solutions to the problems of living on the surface of the earth. Insects swarm in deserts as well as forests. They swim below water and crawl in dark caves. They fly over the high peaks of the Himalayas and even exist on the icecaps of the Poles. One fly makes its home in pools of crude oil welling up from the ground. Another lives in steaming hot volcanic springs, and some survive being frozen solid. They excavate homes for themselves in the skins of animals and burrow long tunnels within the thickness of a leaf. The number of individual insects seems impossible to count, but there must be around one thousand million thousand million. Put another way, for every human alive, there are about a million insects – and together these insects would weigh about 12 times as much as a human does.

There are about three times as many species of insect as of all other kinds of animal put together. So far, scientists have identified about 700,000 of them and there are certainly three or four times as many still unnamed.

Yet all these different insects share the same design: a body divided into three parts – a head bearing the mouth and most of the sense organs; a thorax filled with muscles to move the three pairs of legs beneath and one or two pairs of wings above; and an abdomen containing the organs needed for digestion and reproduction. All three sections have an external skeleton like the shell of the trilobites and crustaceans.

Three of the many insect shapes
The mantis (*top*) with long front legs for seizing its prey, the grasshopper (*above*) with long hind legs for jumping, and the beetle (*below*) with horns it uses for fighting, all have six legs and a three-part body. They are all insects.

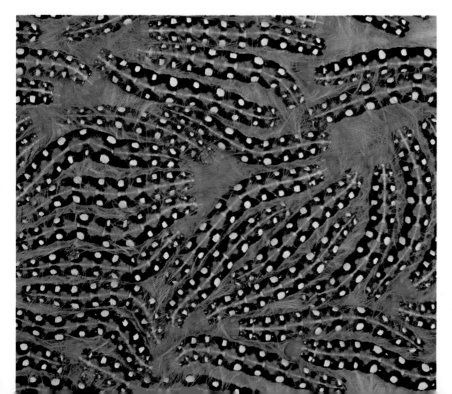

Larvae
Some insects, before they reach their final shape, go through a stage when they look very different. They are then called larvae. These caterpillars (*left*) are the larvae of butterflies.

The coal forests

Coal is the buried remains of forests that grew in swamps some 300 million years ago. The trees were the ancestors of modern horsetails and clubmosses. Some kinds grew to 30 m or more high. When they died, they fell into the water and formed thick deposits of peat. As the course of the creeks shifted, so sand was laid down on top of the peat, squashing it. Eventually the pressure was so great that after millions of years, the peat turned to coal. Within it, the fossilized remains of the animal inhabitants of these

swamps can still be found. Some of them are pictured here. On the fallen trunk of a giant clubmoss tree perches a huge dragonfly, with a wingspan of 70 cm, the largest insect so far discovered. Small cockroaches crawl beside it on the trunk. On the fronds of fern on the right are two flying insects which, like the dragonfly, preyed on other insects. Two amphibians, the first backboned creatures to move onto land, are also here. One (*far left*) is four-legged. Another (*bottom left*) has lost its legs as some modern amphibians have.

Insect armies

An external skeleton is an unexpandable prison. The insects solved the problem of growth in the same way as the trilobites did and crustaceans still do – by moulting. Primitive insects like bristletails and springtails do not change their shape very much as they grow. They merely moult as they increase in size. The ancient winged insects – cockroaches, cicadas, crickets and dragonflies – also grow in a similar way. Their early forms, or larvae, closely resemble the adults except that they lack wings. These only appear after the final moult.

More advanced insects, however, go through dramatic changes. Maggots turn into flies, grubs into beetles, and caterpillars into butterflies. The job of a grub, a maggot or a caterpillar is simply to eat. Its body serves only this one purpose. Since it will not breed in this form, it has no sexual organs. As its parents always place it where it is surrounded by great quantities of food, it needs no wings. Its one essential tool is a pair of jaws. Behind these it needs little more than a

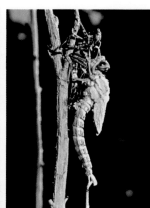

The emergence of a dragonfly
A dragonfly hatches into a larva which lives underwater in a lake or a pond. After two years, or even longer, the larva climbs up a reed out of the water (*above*). Its skin splits and the adult dragonfly clambers out (*above right*). Its crumpled wings slowly expand until eventually the insect is perfect (*right*).

bag of stretchable skin. When this can expand no further, a new soft one forms underneath. The old one then splits and is rolled off, like a stocking from a leg.

These larvae cannot hop, skip or jump. Indeed, they can barely manage to run, for they have only soft ballooning tubes to serve as stumpy legs. But these are quite efficient enough to move the eating machines from one mouthful to another.

The lack of a shell leaves the larvae unprotected. This does not matter to grubs and maggots, for they are hidden from the world while gobbling their way through an apple or gnawing tunnels in wood. But caterpillars, which feed out in the open, need to protect themselves.

They are superb camouflage artists. Some look like twigs, others like bird droppings. If disguises are seen through, many caterpillars have a second line of defence. The pussmoth caterpillar rears its scarlet face and squirts acid to frighten enemies.

Caterpillars of the cinnabar moth

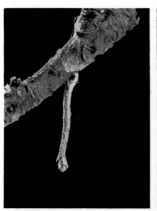   

The defences of caterpillars
The soft-bodied caterpillars defend themselves in many ways. The pussmoth (*left*) squirts acid at its attackers and waves the feelers on the end of its tail. Others (*from left to right above*) hide from enemies with disguises: the orchard moth as a twig, the swallowtail as a bird dropping, and the Assam silk moth and the privet hawkmoth as the leaves of the trees on which they feed.

Insect armies

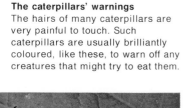

The caterpillars' warnings
The hairs of many caterpillars are very painful to touch. Such caterpillars are usually brilliantly coloured, like these, to warn off any creatures that might try to eat them.

A bagworm
This moth caterpillar protects itself by building a case of fibres as soon as it hatches. It lives inside this while it feeds and eventually turns into a pupa within the case.

Some caterpillars have made themselves unpleasant to eat. They are covered with poisonous hairs and are brilliantly coloured in reds, yellows, blacks and purples – to warn hunters that they are not worth eating. Some harmless caterpillars copy the colours of poisonous ones to protect themselves.

Many insects spend nearly all their lives as such larvae, growing bigger and storing food. Beetle grubs may spend seven years boring through wood and feeding. Caterpillars munch for months, packing away their favourite leaves before the season finishes. But sooner or later, they all reach their full size and the end of their time as larvae.

Now comes the first of two amazing transformations. It is a change some make in private. Insects only have silk glands when they are larvae. They may have used them already to build tents or to make ropes to let themselves down from one twig to another. Now many spin silk to hide themselves from the world. The silk moth caterpillar surrounds itself with a fuzzy bundle of threads, the moon moth constructs a silvery metallic cocoon, the ermine moth builds an elegant casing of lacy net. Many butterfly larvae produce no covering at all. They simply spin a silken sling to attach themselves to a twig.

The life of a pasha butterfly
(*Top left to right*) the egg; the caterpillar; the pupa; (*bottom left to right*) the pupa cracks open; the crumpled adult emerges; the adult, its body expanded and dried.

A silk moth caterpillar spinning
These caterpillars produce the natural silk from which cloth is made.

As soon as they are settled, they discard their caterpillar costumes. Their skin splits, revealing a smooth, brown, hard-shelled object, the pupa. It has openings along its side through which it can breathe, but it does not feed. Its life seems to have come to a standstill. Inside, however, enormous changes are taking place. The entire body of the larvae is being broken down and reassembled in a completely different form.

This new creature usually emerges from the shell of the old during the night. A butterfly pupa, hanging from a twig, begins to shake. A head with two eyes and antennae pushes through the pupa at one end. Legs come free and begin clawing frantically in the air. Slowly, the insect hauls itself out. On its back are two flat wrinkled wings. The insect jerks itself free and hangs on the empty pupa case, its body trembling. It begins to pump blood into the veins in the wings. Slowly they expand. Within half an hour the wings are fully spread. Gradually the veins harden to give the wings their strength. All this time, the wings have been held together like the leaves of a book. Now, as they dry and become stiff, the insect slowly moves them apart to show the world for the first time the perfection of their shimmering colours.

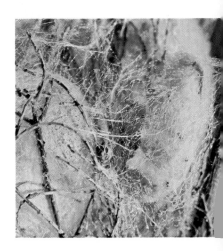

Insect armies

The varied patterns of butterfly wings
(*Top*) bee butterfly with transparent wings from Trinidad; (*right*) brimstone from Europe; (*below*) eyespot butterfly from South America; (*bottom*) monarch butterfly from North America.

The insect has now used up most of the food that it gathered when it was a larva. For the adult, feeding is of little importance. Mayflies and some moths do not even have mouth-parts. Others sip nectar during their brief lives to give them energy, but none need to feed in order to build their bodies. Their growth has come to an end. The goal now is to find a mate.

Butterflies do so by displaying their wings to attract mates. Unlike their larvae, butterflies have excellent eyes and their dazzling wings are the most elaborate visual signals.

Other insects use other ways to signal to each other. Cicadas, crickets and grasshoppers rely on sound. Most insects are deaf, so these groups have had to develop not only voices but ears. Cicadas have eardrums on either side of the thorax while grasshoppers have them on their legs. Some grasshoppers produce their whirring trills by sawing the notched edge of their hind legs against their wings. Such calls make it possible for an individual to identify the presence of another of its own species. So a male can avoid the territory of another singing male, and a female fly towards it.

The flight of butterflies and moths
Butterflies and moths have large
and fragile wings but are
nonetheless skilled flyers. Most,
like the eighty-nine butterfly (*left*),
can fly at about 9 km/h. The
hummingbird hawkmoth (*above*)
can fly at 18 km/h and even hover
in front of flowers to sip nectar. The
patterns on their wings are
produced by tiny scales, like these
(*below left*) on the wing of a
swallowtail.

The antennae of an atlas moth
The female atlas moth attracts the
male by smell. The male (*below*)
has large feathery antennae with
which he can detect her scent,
even many kilometres away.

Insect armies

Other insects attract their mates by smell. The females of some moths produce an odour that the males can detect with large feathery antennae. These organs are so sensitive and the scent is so powerful that a female has been known to summon a male from 11 km away.

So, by sight, sound and smell, the adult insects attract their mates. Male grasps female while mating. The couple may even fly through the air, awkwardly linked together. Then the female lays her fertilized eggs and provides food for them. Butterflies seek out the one plant whose leaves provide the only food their caterpillars will

Insects mating
The male and females of many insects, like grasshoppers (*above*), weevils (*far right*) and beetles (*below left*) come together and may stay clasped in pairs for some time. Others have more complicated methods. Houseflies (*below right*) mate while flying. In dragonflies and damselflies (*above right*) the male first deposits his sperm into a special pocket on his underside close to his legs. He then holds the female at the back of her neck with claspers at the end of his abdomen while she reaches forward with her abdomen to collect the sperm.

eat. Beetles bury pellets of dung and lay their eggs within them. Flies deposit their eggs on meat. Solitary wasps catch spiders, paralyse them with a sting and stack them around their eggs so that the young larvae will have fresh meat awaiting them. The female ichneumon wasp has an egg-laying organ like a drill with which she bores a hole in wood where she has detected a beetle grub lying beneath. She pierces it and deposits an egg in its soft body. Her larva, when it hatches, will eat the grub alive. And so the whole process of egg-larva-pupa-adult begins once more.

Insect eggs

Food must be near a young insect when it emerges from its egg. The harlequin bug (*left*) lays her eggs on the stem of the food plant; the flesh fly (*above*) on a dead mammal such as a vole, for her maggots eat carrion. The parasitic wasp (*below*) puts her egg inside a caterpillar, and the scarab beetle (*bottom*) collects a ball of dung as food for her young.

A queen termite
(*Top*) she is many times bigger than the worker termites which not only bring her food but also collect the eggs (*above*).

Compass termites
In Australia, the compass termites build their nests always pointing north and south. This probably helps prevent them from becoming overheated during the middle of the day.

The insect body has produced an almost infinite variety of forms. The only limit seems to be size. The largest living insects today are not longer than about 30 cm. But the insects have a way of overcoming their small size. All over the tropics stand termite hills. A single hill contains a colony of several million insects. They are not just creatures that have chosen to live together in one communal dwelling, like human beings in some gigantic tower block. For one thing they are all one family, the offspring of a single pair of adults. For another, all of them are incomplete creatures, incapable of living on their own. The workers, scurrying along the tracks through the undergrowth, are blind and cannot breed. The soldiers that stand guard beside the entrances and defend any breach in the walls are armed with jaws so huge that they can no longer gather food for themselves and have to be fed by the workers. At the centre of the colony lies the queen. She is imprisoned within thick walls from which she can never escape, for her body is far too big to get through the passages that lead to it. Her abdomen is swollen into a white heaving sausage, 12 cm long, from which she produces eggs at the rate of 30,000 a day. She too would die if she were not cared for. Teams of workers deliver food to her at one end and collect eggs from the other. The only sexually active male, the wasp-sized king, stays alongside her and he too is fed by the workers.

The link that binds all these individuals together is a highly effective system of communication. Soldier termites sound an alarm by beating their large hard heads on passage walls. Workers, discovering a new source of food, leave a scent trail which their blind fellows can easily follow. But the most important means of communicating is by chemical messages. All the members of the colony continually exchange food and spit or saliva with one another which contain these messages. So instructions are circulated through-

out the colony with great speed.

At certain times in the colony's life, the larvae develop into sexually mature adults. Then the workers open special slits in the sides of the mound and flying termites pour out of the openings into the sky. They seldom go far. They come down onto the ground and their wings break off. Those few termites that escape being eaten by birds and lizards form pairs and go off together to find a nest site in a crack in the ground or in a tree. There they build a small royal cell. Within it, they mate and lay eggs and a new colony is born.

Termites are closely related to those ancient insects, the cockroaches. Like them, their bodies do not have waists and the young larvae are similar to the adult winged form. They grow by a series of moults but never pass through a pupal stage or undergo a major transformation. Like cockroaches, too, termites feed mostly on vegetable matter, such as twigs, leaves and grass. Some specialize in eating timber, boring away inside wood until it becomes a hollow shell that collapses at the touch of a finger.

One other group of insects has taken to the colonial life like the termites – the wasps, bees and ants. Each of these has a narrow waist, two pairs of transparent wings and a powerful sting. Wasps still show the stages by which colonialism may have developed. Some hunting wasps live entirely on their own. The female, after mating, builds her own mud cells, lays an egg in each, provides it with a collection of paralysed spiders for food and then abandons it. In other species, the female stays beside the nest and when the young hatch, she brings food to them day after day. In yet others, the females build their nests close to one another but, after a few weeks, some abandon their own nests and join others in building theirs. Eventually, one female becomes dominant and lays all the eggs while the others build cells and collect food for her.

Termite nests
In wet areas, like the African rain forest, termites build roofs to their nests (*above left*). In drier parts of Africa, they construct towers 3 or 4 m high (*above*). Other kinds make turrets around their nests which act as ventilation shafts (*below*).

Worker bees tending their queen
She is the slightly bigger insect in the centre.

The honeybees live in colonies of many thousands. The single queen stays on the wax combs, laying eggs in the cells that have been built by the workers. The community, like that of the termites, is bound together by a system of chemical messages circulating within the hive. But bees have other ways of communicating between one another. Flying through the air to find food, they cannot leave scent trails on the ground as termites do. Instead, they dance.

When a worker bee arrives back in the hive after finding a flower, it performs a special dance on the landing platform in front of the entrance to the colony. First it scurries round in a circle, then it crosses it, waggling its abdomen and buzzing. This track points directly to the source of food. Workers immediately fly off in the direction shown. When they return with the honey, they too will perform a dance so that, in a very short time, most of the work force in the hive is gathering honey from the new source.

The life of honeybees
(*Top left*) a cross-section of the comb showing the long white eggs; (*top right*) a cross-section of the comb showing the developing pupae in the cells; (*middle left*) pupae in their cells; (*middle right*) sealed cells in the comb containing larvae; (*bottom left*) workers hatching from the cells; (*bottom right*) workers on the comb.

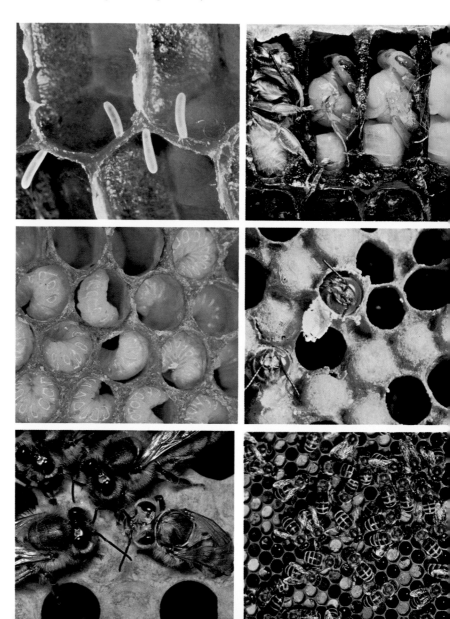

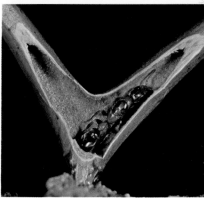

The most complex colonies in the insect world are those created by the ants. Some live within plants – in galls, hollow stems or thorns with swollen bases. The leaf-cutting ants of South America build vast underground nests where they grow a fungus for food. Tree ants in southeast Asia construct nests by sewing leaves together using silk produced by the larvae. In Australia, the honeypot ants collect nectar and force-feed it to a special type of worker ant until their abdomens are swollen to the size of peas and their skins stretched so thin that they are quite transparent. The workers then hang them up by their front legs so that they are like living storage jars.

Most ants, however, are carnivorous. Many prey upon termites, raiding the great mounds and doing battle with the soldiers. If they win, they devour the defenceless workers and larvae. Others make slaves of different ants. They raid the nest, collect the pupae and carry them back to their own colony. When these hatch, the young ants serve their captors, collecting food and feeding it to them.

The most terrifying of all ants are those that make no nest but wander through the countryside seeking prey. In South America they are known as army ants, in Africa as drivers. They march in columns so long they may take several hours to pass one spot. At the head, the soldiers fan out to look for food. Behind comes a column of workers, many of them carrying larvae. When the hunters at the head of the column discover prey, they swarm all over it, cutting it apart. Grasshoppers, scorpions, lizards, young birds in their nests, anything that cannot get out of the way is attacked. In west Africa any animal which is tied up may be attacked by one of these armies. I once made a large collection of snakes there. We had Gaboon vipers, puff adders, spitting cobras as well as harmless species like tree snakes and pythons. We kept them in a mud-walled hut and posted a guard to keep watch, armed with a can of paraffin. Only that, poured on the ground and set alight, will turn a raiding column of ants. In spite of all precautions, one afternoon a column got into the hut through a

Insect armies

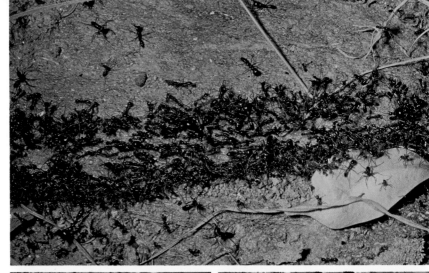

hole in the wall at the back. By the time we had discovered what had happened, the ants were swarming over the snakes. Infuriated by the painful bites, the snakes were striking madly and uselessly at their tiny attackers. Every one had to be taken out and held down while we picked off the ants that were sinking their jaws between the scales. In spite of all we could do, several snakes died from the ant bites.

Army ants march and hunt for weeks, day after day. When it is time for the larvae to pupate, the army makes camp. There may be as many as 150,000 ants and they cluster in a ball between the roots of a tree or beneath an overhanging stone. Clinging to one another, they make a living nest from their bodies, complete with passageways and chambers for the queen and the pupae. During the next few days, the queen lays as many as 25,000 eggs. They hatch very quickly and at the same time a new generation of workers and soldiers emerge from the stored pupae. Soon the army is ready to march off to war again with its ranks swollen by these new recruits.

The insects colonized the land before the vertebrates and they still exploit every living thing on it. There is no known species of plant that is not attacked in one way or another by them. Not only do insects rob us of our food, but they suck our blood, bury themselves in our skin and infect us with all kinds of serious diseases. In return, we attack them with flame-throwers and spray them with chemical poisons. And yet, in spite of all our efforts, we have so far failed to exterminate a single insect species.

5 · The conquest of the waters

The lancelet is an odd and mysterious creature. It is shaped like a slim leaf about 6 cm long and lives half-buried in the sand of the sea floor. Its front end sticks up above the surface and has an opening, ringed with tentacles, through which it sucks in water. Its body is very simple. There is nothing that could be called a head, merely a small light-sensitive spot on the front end; no heart, only a number of throbbing blood vessels; no fins or limbs, only a slight widening at the back end. It has a thin gristly rod in its back which runs the entire length of its body. Muscles are attached to this rod. When the lancelet tightens them, a series of waves runs down its body. These push water backwards and so the lancelet moves forward. It swims. It seems that creatures very like it could have been the ancestors of fish.

Another strange creature may represent a link between the lancelet and true fish. It is somewhat larger than the lancelet. It is found in the rivers of Europe and America where it lives in holes in the mud and filter-feeds. It is jawless, blind and without fins except for a fringe around the tail. For many years it was thought to be an adult creature and was given a special name. Then it was discovered that it is only the larva of a very well known animal – the lamprey.

A lancelet

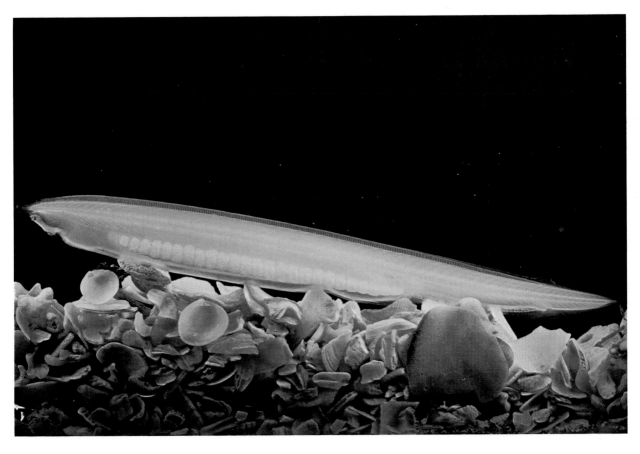

Lampreys feeding on a carp

The mouth of a lamprey

You might be excused for thinking that the adult lamprey is a true fish. But it is not. It has a flexible rod running along its back but it does not have jaws. Its head ends in a large circular disc in the centre of which is a tongue covered with sharp spines. It has two small eyes with a single nostril between them and on either side of its neck, a row of gill slits. With the disc, the lamprey clamps itself on the side of a fish and eats the fish alive. Lampreys may seem unattractive from a human point of view, but they are very interesting, for their ancestors were once the most advanced and revolutionary creatures in the seas. Their remains have now been found in rocks that are about 540 million years old.

These ancient fossil relatives of the lamprey cannot be called true fish either, for they had no jaws. They were mostly quite small, the size of large minnows. and were heavily armoured. Some of them had their heads and bodies covered with bony plates. In front they had two eyes and a single central nostril, like that of a lamprey. At the back, a muscular tail with a fin stuck out from the armour. By beating this, they could drive themselves through the water but their heavy foreparts must have kept their heads low and close to the bottom. Most had no fins at all, apart from their tails, to help them steer. Without jaws, these creatures could not prey upon shelled molluscs. They just nuzzled their way across the sea bottom, sucking up mud and filtering out the edible parts.

However, they survived and increased in numbers and variety. Their heavy armour-plating must have given them much needed protection, for the seas at this time were ruled by huge, 2 m long sea scorpions, armed with enormous claws, which fed on the smaller creatures of the sea floor.

Eventually some appeared that grew to a considerable size, 60 cm or so. Many were quite mobile. A single fin down the mid-line of their backs or undersides prevented them from spinning in the water and helped steady them, but none had paired side fins. So none of

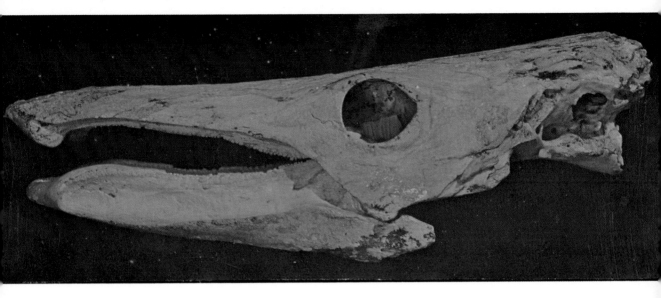

them were really efficient swimmers.

The situation remained like this for 100 million years. During this immensity of time, the corals arrived and began to build reefs, and the jointed animals developed into forms that soon would leave the sea for the land. Important changes also took place among the jawless fish. The slits in the sides of their throats used to filter food became gills. Rods of bone developed below the mouths and turned into jaws. The skin covering the jaws had bony scales in it. These grew much larger and sharper and became teeth. These creatures did not merely sift mud. Now they could bite. Flaps of skin grew out of either side of the lower part of the body, helping to guide them through the water, and became fins. Now these creatures could swim. And so, for the first time, fish began to move with skill and accuracy through the waters of the sea.

It is possible to walk across the sea bed of that time, 400 million years ago. In the flat desert land of northwestern Australia, close to a place called Gogo by the Aborigines, rises a line of strange, steep-sided rocky bluffs, 300 m high. Geologists discovered that the rocks were full of the remains of coral. Once sea had covered this area and these cliffs were reefs, bordering deep fish-filled lagoons. On what was once the sea floor, lie lumps of rock with bones sticking out of them. The geologists took the lumps back to the laboratory and soaked them for months in weak acid. Gradually the rock fell away and exposed the first complete skeletons of the world's earliest true fish.

There were many different kinds. Most were armoured in some way, with heavy scales attached to bony plates in the skin, and they had fearsome teeth in their jaws. They also had a bony skeleton with the beginnings of a bony spine. All of them had well-developed side fins, usually in two pairs, one pair just behind the throat, and the other near the anus. In the face of competition from these new fish, nearly all the jawless fish died out.

The first true fish

This painting shows an underwater scene in one of the lagoons that, 350 million years ago, lay in northwestern Australia around the place now known as Gogo. At the back, in the dim distance, rise reefs built by stony corals. Other corals grow in the foreground. A small crustacean crawls over the sea floor at the bottom of the picture in the middle.

Over 20 different species of fish, including all those shown here, have been found as fossils at Gogo. None of them was as skilful at swimming as modern fish. The three big ones in the bottom left-hand corner grew to about 30 cm long. Their front parts and limbs were

covered in a heavy armour of bone. They lived on the bottom and fed by filtering food from the mud. The fish on the right also lived on the bottom, but was probably more choosy in its feeding habits. The big fish in the top right-hand corner, together with the one coming round a coral bluff and the small one half out of the coral cave, are lungfish. There were many species of lungfish at this time. Some used their lungs for breathing but others, like those shown here, relied mostly on their gills. The big fish at the back is an early bony fish, a member of the great group of fish that is today the most abundant.

Sharks

There are about 250 different kinds of sharks alive today. The white-tip reef shark (*above*) is about 1.5 m long and harmless to humans. The great white shark (*below*), however, can be a man-eater and grows to 10 m long. Because sharks have no swim bladder, they sometimes rest by lying on the sea floor (*bottom*).

At about this time, a definite split appeared among fish. One group developed which lost nearly all the bone in their skeletons but developed instead cartilage, a softer, lighter material. They were the ancestors of today's sharks and rays. Without heavy bone they were lighter than their bony relatives. Even so, flesh and cartilage is heavier than water and to remain above the sea floor, the ancient sharks had to keep swimming just as their descendants do today.

Sharks drive themselves through the water by wriggling the rear halves of their bodies and thrashing their tails. But with the thrust coming from the back, the body is nose-heavy and tends to dive downwards. To correct this, the shark has two breast fins spread horizontally like the wings of a rear-engined aircraft. The shark cannot move them very much or suddenly twist them into position to act as brakes. Indeed, a charging shark cannot stop, it can only swerve away to one side. Nor can it swim backwards. Furthermore, if it stops beating its tail, it sinks. Some sharks take rests at night and sleep on the sea floor.

Rays and skates, relatives of the sharks with skeletons of cartilage like them, have taken to bottom-living more or less permanently. Their bodies have become greatly flattened, their side fins enlarged into huge triangles which they flap to move themselves forwards. Their tails need no longer beat to keep them afloat and have become thin and whip-like. Sometimes they have a poisonous spine at the end. Rays cannot swim fast but they do not need to do so. They are not hunters. Their mouths open on the underside of their bodies, and most live on molluscs and crustaceans which they grub up from the sea floor.

One kind of ray, the manta, has gone back to swimming in the surface waters. Its side fins enable it to remain aloft with little effort, using the water for support as gliders use air. But side fins are not so powerful as the thrashing tail, so the manta cannot swim as fast as its shark cousins. Instead it sails slowly through the water on flapping wing-like fins, sometimes as much as 7 m across, with its immense slot-like mouth wide open, filtering crustaceans and small fish.

Rays
The huge manta ray (*above and below*) swims near the surface, but most rays live on the bottom like the cowtail ray (*bottom left*) and the sting ray (*bottom right*).

A pike pouncing

Mackerel

The second great group of fish kept bone in their skeletons and it is their descendants that today rule the waters of the world. They solved the problem of weight, in a roundabout way. During the early period several families spread from the open seas into coastal waters and eventually into shallow lagoons and swamps. Breathing for a fish is difficult in such places, because the warmer water becomes, the less oxygen it contains. So when fish came to live there, they had to develop additional ways of getting oxygen. The bichir, a fish of ancient ancestry which lives in the rivers and swamps of Africa, still uses the method they adopted. It rises to the surface of the water and takes a gulp of air. This goes down its throat and into a pouch that opens from the top of its gut. The walls of the pouch are thick with blood vessels which absorb gaseous oxygen. So the bichir not only has gills like any other fish, but a simple lung as well. An air-filled pouch has other advantages. It enables the fish to keep afloat without constantly thrashing its tail. Eventually bony fish with these air pouches appeared in the sea.

Soon species developed which could fill their air pouches by producing gas from the blood rather than by rising to the surface and swallowing air. In some cases the tube connecting the pouch to the gut became no more than a solid thread. So the fish acquired a swim bladder. Because a fish could now control its level in the water by

The end of the pike's hunt

using its swim bladder, its breast fins were free to give it fine control of movement and the techniques of swimming changed.

Water is 800 times as dense as air, and the slightest bump on the body of a fish can cause drag, more even than it would on a bird or an aeroplane. So the high-speed fish – tuna, bonito, marlin, mackerel – have streamlined bodies, sharply pointed in the front, swelling quickly to the greatest width and then tapering elegantly to the tail fin. The whole of the rear half of the fish is the engine for this propeller. Muscles attached to the backbone enable the tail to be beaten from side to side with unflagging strength. The scales, so heavy and rough in early fish, have now become thin and smoothly fitting or have been lost altogether. The surface of the body is slippery. The plate covering the gills fits closely to the body and the eyes barely bulge above the smooth outlines. The side fins work as rudders or brakes. When the fish is moving at speed and they are not needed, they are clamped to the fish's side.

Not all fish have adopted a life of speed. Those living in mid-water or along the shores have different problems and needs. The pike uses its fins as oars, rotating them slowly back and forth so that the fish can remain still in the water and hang above a rock despite the current. The dragonfish has expanded its fins into defensive weapons, each ray spiked with poison. Several species have once again taken to

Dragonfish

The conquest of the waters

Two armoured fish
The sea horse (*below*) is only about 10 cm long. It is a poor swimmer, like its relative, the weedy sea dragon (*right*). Both propel themselves when they have to by waving the fins on their backs.

A flounder
Like its relatives, the plaice, the sole and the halibut, the flounder (*right*) lies on its side on the sea floor. It can change the colour of its upper side to match its background and so hide itself (*far right*).

armour since body weight is no longer such a problem. The boxfish, safely enclosed in a case of bones just beneath its skin, sails confidently over the dangerous world of the reef. The sea horse is also armoured. Its tail has no fin on it but is used as a hook with which the fish anchors itself to weed or coral. Its body is held upright and what was the fin on the top of its back has become a rear engine with which it can move upright through the corals and weed forests.

Some bony fish, such as the flounder and the plaice, have copied the skates and rays and taken to bottom-living. When it first hatches, the flounder swims above the sea floor in a normal way. After a few months, it undergoes a transformation. It loses the swim bladder it has had until now. Its head becomes twisted and the mouth moves sideways. One eye shifts right round the body so that it is alongside the other. Then the fish goes down to the bottom and lies on its side. The breast fins are now of little use, though the fish still keeps them. It swims by waving its much enlarged fins that originally ran along the top of its back and below its underside.

So, driven by their beating tails, sculled by their breast fins, gliding on side fins, the fish swim with speed and accuracy through all parts of the sea. But if you travel, you must know where you are going.

All fish have one sense which we do not have. Down their sides runs a little line with a slightly different texture from the rest of the body. It is made up of a number of holes or pores by which the fish can detect differences of pressure in the water. As it swims, a fish creates a pressure wave that travels ahead of it. When this meets some other object, the fish can sense the change. This ability to feel at a distance is very important for fish that swim in groups or shoals.

The fish has an excellent sense of smell. Sharks can smell blood at a distance of nearly half a kilometre. Fish can also hear well. Sound travels better in water than in air. Because the fish's body contains a lot of water the sound waves can enter the skull and reach the inner 'ear' without the special outside opening that land vertebrates have.

Sight was also an ability acquired very early. The lancelet's eyespot makes it aware of the difference between light and dark. The jawless fish had eyes that peered through chinks in their armour. There are only a few basic designs for an efficient eye. One is the mosaic eye developed by trilobites and kept by the insects. Another is a closed chamber with a window and a lens in front and a light-sensitive back. This is the pattern of the squid and octopus eye as well as of the mechanical eye built by humans, the camera. It is also the basis of the eye developed by the fish and passed on by them to all land vertebrates.

The eyes of almost all sharks and rays lack the kind of cells at the back that are needed for seeing colour. Not surprisingly, therefore, these fish are themselves drab creatures dressed in browns and greys, olive green and steel blue. When they are patterned, their designs tend to be simple spots and dapples. Bony fish, on the other hand, are strikingly different. Their eyes can see colour well and their body colours are bright and varied.

A boxfish
There are many different kinds of boxfish. This one, with its two long bony horns, is often called a cowfish.

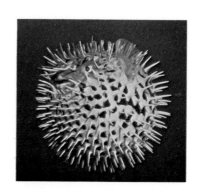

A puffer fish
When threatened, this fish swallows water or air and blows itself up into a thorny ball, far too big and spiny to be swallowed by any hunter.

The conquest of the waters

The most brilliantly patterned fish of all are those fish that live in clear sunlit waters around coral reefs where their designs are easily seen. There is a huge and crowded population here because of the richness of food. Therefore it becomes very important that the various species can be told apart and so each has developed its own distinctive different colour and pattern.

At spawning time, male fish often adopt particularly brilliant colours to threaten rivals and attract females. As they become excited, they fight with their colours, circling one another, flexing and quivering their fins. They beat their tails and tear at the patterns on one another's fins. Eventually when one has had enough, he signals surrender by changing the patterns on his skin. The winner is now free to court his female. He then uses much the same show of colours and patterns and fin displays as he did for fighting to encourage the female to lay her eggs.

Flying fish
When alarmed, they leap from the surface of the water and spread their huge front pair of fins to form gliding wings. They can then glide above the waves for hundreds of metres.

A change of costume
This male cichlid fish from Africa develops his bright colours and stripes only during the courtship season.

The varied patterns of butterfly fish (*opposite page*)

Black-blotched butterfly fish

Meyer's butterfly fish

Lineated butterfly fish

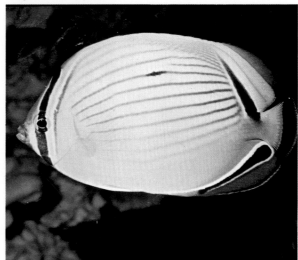

Masked butterfly fish

Saddled butterfly fish

Tinker's butterfly fish

The conquest of the waters

Luminous fish from the deep sea
(*Top right*) a deep-sea anchovy; (*top far right*) a viper fish; (*right*) angler fish; (*bottom*) a hatchet fish.

In the depths of the ocean, around 750 m and below, there is no light by which fish can see one another's signals, so many make their own. Some produce winks and flashes of light. These are signals of some kind – messages to the rest of the shoal, calls to mates – but we do not know a great deal about their use. The deep-sea angler fish uses light to catch its food. It has a fin ray which droops over the front of the mouth with a glowing green bulb at the end. When other fish come to investigate this swaying light, the angler suddenly opens its huge mouth – and gulps one more meal.

Some fish living in the dark waters of tropical rivers have developed a method of finding their way about that no other creature so far has copied. They make electricity within their bodies and send out electrical signals. These signals send patterns of current into the surrounding water. Any object in the water will distort the pattern and the fish notices the changes.

The largest of such fish is the South American electric eel. It grows to 1.5 m in length and as thick as a human's arm. Often it makes its

An electric eel

home in holes beneath a river bank or among rocks. Backing into these holes, for a lengthy creature like an eel, causes steering problems. The eel solves them with the help of electricity. If you watch one tackling such a problem in a tank and listen to the electrical signals it makes on a special loudspeaker, you can hear how it sends out increasing numbers of signals as it identifies the outlines of the parking place behind it and then slowly moves into it without once touching the sides. But the electric eel has another set of batteries that produce not steady low-voltage discharges, but sudden shocks so strong that if you pick up such a fish without the insulation of rubber gloves and boots, it can throw you flat on your back. It is one of the very few creatures that can kill by electrocution.

Today, 500 million years after those jawless armoured creatures began to wag their tails and blunder over the muddy bottoms of the ancient sea, the fish have developed into some 30,000 different species. They have colonized every part of the seas, lakes and rivers of the world.

A scaly dragon fish
This fish lives in the darkness of the deep sea and finds its way around with a feeler under its chin.

The conquest of the waters

Salmon leaping a waterfall

Male Pacific salmon fighting

Salmon eggs in gravel

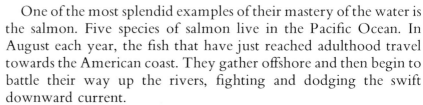

One of the most splendid examples of their mastery of the water is the salmon. Five species of salmon live in the Pacific Ocean. In August each year, the fish that have just reached adulthood travel towards the American coast. They gather offshore and then begin to battle their way up the rivers, fighting and dodging the swift downward current.

These rivers are not chosen at random. The salmon remember the precise taste of the waters in which they hatched. This memory draws them across several hundred miles of ocean, brings them to a particular bay and, as the scent gets stronger and stronger, up one special river and into one particular stream. We know that it is smell that guides them, for salmon with their nostrils blocked get lost.

The urge to return may be strong, but the obstacles are huge. On their way upstream, the salmon may have to leap up waterfalls. Eventually they reach the shallow stretches where their parents spawned and they lie there resting. Within a few days, their bodies change. They develop humps on their backs. Their upper jaws become hooked and their teeth grow into long fangs. These teeth are for battle. The males wrestle and fight, flank to flank, seizing one another's jaws, striking at their opponents with their bared teeth. At last, one wins and a female joins him. Swiftly eggs and sperm are deposited and sink beneath the gravel. Now the adults are totally exhausted and soon they die. Not a single one of the millions of fish that fought their way up the river ever returns to the sea.

But in the gravel, the eggs remain, 1000 or so from every female. They stay safe throughout the winter. Next spring they hatch. The small fish, or fry, remain in the streams for a few weeks, feeding on insects and crustaceans, before following the current downstream to the sea. They will swim there for many seasons, but eventually the survivors will fight their way back up their own river to spawn and die in the very place where they were hatched.

Three-quarters of the world's surface is covered by water. Three-quarters of the world belongs to the fish.

6 · The invasion of the land

One of the most important events in the history of life took place some 350 million years ago in a freshwater swamp. Fish began to haul themselves out of water and live on the land. To cross this frontier, they had to solve two problems: first, how to move around out of water, and second, how to obtain oxygen from the air.

One living fish manages to do both these things today – the mudskipper. Mudskippers are only a few centimetres long and you can find them in mangrove swamps in the tropics, lying on the glistening mud beyond the lap of the waters. Some cling to the roots of the mangroves or clamber up trunks. They come out to feed on the insects and other animals that swarm on the soft oozy surface of the mud. They often move by flicking their tails so that they give little skipping jumps. But they can also edge themselves forwards with their front pair of fins. The fins have fleshy bases with strong bones inside which help support their weight. Such limblike fins are a little like those of the primitive bony fish that were living when the move to land was first made. The most famous of these is the coelacanth.

The first coelacanths were found as fossils over a century ago. Most were about 400 million years old. None were younger than 70 million years. They were studied with great care because it seemed likely that they were the creatures from which the first land animals with backbones were descended. But since coelacanths had become extinct long ago, scientists thought they would never know exactly how they moved and breathed.

Then, in 1938, a trawler fishing off the coast of South Africa brought up a very strange fish. It was large, nearly 2 m long, with

A mudskipper

A living coelacanth

The invasion of the land

powerful jaws and heavy armoured scales. A specialist on African fish was called to see it, but before he got to it, its insides had rotted and had to be thrown away. However, he recognized it immediately as a coelacanth and informed the world that a creature thought to have been extinct for 70 million years was still alive.

It was a scientific sensation and a huge search for another specimen was mounted. But without success. Then, 14 years later, another was caught – not off South Africa but nearly 1500 km away, in the Indian Ocean near the tiny Comoro Islands. The first coelacanth must have been stray, for the fishermen of the Comores said that they regularly caught such fish. Since that time, several dozen more coelacanths have been caught but they very seldom reach the shore alive. Many expeditions have gone to the Comores hoping to catch a living specimen. We too went there and searched for them, night after night, but without success. Then just before the last of us left the island a fisherman brought one in, lashed to the side of his canoe. It, too, was nearly dead. But he released it in a bay long enough for it to be filmed with an underwater camera as it swam slowly above the bottom. It held its stout forefins away from the sides of its body. Had it been stronger it could have used them to help it move over the rocky sea floor. So such fleshy fins might well have enabled a fish to move about on land.

But what solution could the early fish find to the problem of breathing out of water? The mudskipper has a way of getting oxygen from a mouthful of water by swilling it around and absorbing the oxygen it contains through the lining of the mouth. It also absorbs some oxygen from the air through its moist skin. But still it can only remain out of water for a short time. Within a few minutes it has to return to wet its skin and take a fresh mouthful of water. Nor can the living coelacanth suggest an answer to the problem, for today it never leaves its deep waters. There is, however, another living fish that has a solution.

An African lungfish

An Australian lungfish

Many African swamps turn to hard sun-baked mud during the dry season. Yet the lungfish manages to live in them. It survives by breathing air. As the pools shrink, the lungfish digs into the mud. It curls into a ball, wrapping its tail around its head, and lines its hole with slime. As the mud dries, the slime forms a dry skin. It has left a tube through the mud so that air can reach pouches that open from the back of its throat. These are simple lungs. With their help, the lungfish can breathe. So it survives for months, even years. When the rains do finally return and water fills the pond again, the fish comes to life. It wriggles free of its cocoon and swims off. In the water, it breathes with its gills like a normal fish, but it uses lungs too, rising now and then to gulp air from the surface. Four different kinds of lungfish are found in Africa, one in Australia and another in South America. They were, however, like the coelacanth, much more common 350 million years ago.

Between them, the lungfish and the coelacanth have the two basic abilities that the first land-exploring fish needed – the ability to breathe air and to move on land. But the shape of the bones of their skulls are so different from those of the first land vertebrates that neither could be their ancestors.

However, a third fish, called Eusthenopteron, was living at the same period. It had leglike fins like the coelacanth. It also seems very likely that it had air-breathing pouches like a lungfish. Its skull, however, has the important feature which neither the coelacanth nor the lungfish has – a passage linking its nostrils with the roof of its mouth. All land vertebrates have this feature and it is this which confirms that this fish is indeed very closely related to the creatures which gave rise to the first land-living backboned creatures.

But why should the descendants of Eusthenopteron have clambered onto the land? Perhaps, like the lungfish of today, they lived in pools that were seasonal and used their lungs and legs to search for other water when their homes went dry. Perhaps, like the mud-

A swamp 350 million years ago
This painting shows Eusthenopteron on the left, hauling itself out of the water using its leglike front fins. On the dry land, ahead of it, stands one of the first four-legged land animals, an early amphibian about 4 m long. The plants around it are the huge ancestors of today's clubmosses and horsetails.

Amphibians with tails
There are about 450 different kinds
of newts and salamanders. The
red-spotted newt (*above*) comes
from North America, the Alpine
newt (*right*) and the warty newt
(*below*) from Europe.

skipper, they were tempted out by new sources of food on land.
Maybe it was because there were no other creatures on land that might
attack them. Perhaps it was a combination of all these reasons.
Whatever it was that lured or drove them there, over the years these
creatures became more skilful at moving and breathing out of water.

The swamps through which they waddled were thick with great
horsetail and clubmoss trees. These, when fossilized, formed coal,
and it is in coal seams that we find the bones of these first vertebrate
inhabitants of the land, the amphibians.

For the next 100 million years the amphibians ruled the land.
Some of them must have been terrifying. They grew to 3 or 4 m long
and their jaws were spiked with sharp teeth. The amphibians living
today that most closely resemble these early ones are the salamanders
and newts. The largest lives in the rivers of Japan. It grows to
about 1.5 m – only a quarter of the size of its ancestors but much
larger than other amphibians today. A newt is only about 10 cm long,
but has the same body shape – long, with four small legs and a tail.

The newt spends most of its time on land. It hides beneath stones
or in damp places searching for the worms, slugs and insects on

which it lives. But it cannot stray far from water. For one thing, it must keep its skin moist to help it breathe, for its lungs are simple and small and do not provide enough oxygen for its needs. Also, the newt, like other amphibians, cannot drink with its mouth. It has to absorb all the water it needs through its skin. If its skin dries out, it will die. But there is a third need that ties an amphibian to water. Its eggs do not have watertight shells, and so they are in danger of drying out on land. So the newt goes back to the water to breed.

In the breeding season, when it lives in the water, the newt becomes quite fishlike. It swims, with its legs tucked out of the way, by wriggling its body and beating its tail. During courtship some males develop a crest along their backs and become brightly coloured as fish do when displaying to the females. The female lays many eggs, attaching each one to the leaf of a water plant. When the young hatch, they are even more fishlike than their parents. They have no legs and breathe not with lungs, which will develop later, but with feathery outside gills. They are called tadpoles.

In Mexico there is a salamander that remains a tadpole all its life. It even breeds as a tadpole. The Aztecs called it axolotl – a name which

The invasion of the land

means 'water monster' – perhaps because its outside gills grow into great branching bushes on either side of its neck. In the United States, one amphibian has gone back completely to water-living – the mud puppy. It has both gills and lungs, lays its eggs in a nest in the bottom of a stream and remains in water throughout its life.

Some salamanders have returned even more closely to the shape of their fish ancestors. The siren, 1 m long salamander from the southern United States, has lost its back legs and its front legs are so small they are useless.

One group of amphibians have lost all their legs. They are called caecilians and live mostly in the tropics, burrowing underground. They have long thin bodies and no legs. Caecilians might be mistaken for brightly coloured earthworms. But unlike earthworms, the caecilians are meat-eaters. They can be quite alarming if you think you are handling a harmless worm, for they may suddenly open their huge hunters' jaws.

There are about 160 kinds of caecilians known and about 300 kinds of salamanders and newts, but by far the most numerous amphibians alive today belong to a third group, the frogs and toads. There are about 2600 of them.

In temperate parts of the world, we distinguish between frogs

An amphibian without legs
A caecilian from Sri Lanka about 45 cm long.

Amphibians without tails
Most frogs, like the European edible frog (*right*), are expert leapers. The South American flying frog (*below*) has huge membranes between its toes which enable it to turn its jumps into glides.

with smooth moist skin and toads with drier more warty skins. The difference, however, is little more than skin deep. In the tropics, there are many in-between forms which could either be called frog or toad. Instead of lengthening their bodies and losing their legs like the caecilians, the frogs and toads have shortened their bodies and developed their legs enormously. The biggest of all, the goliath frog from west Africa, is able to jump 3 m or so. Spectacular though this is, many smaller frogs can easily outdo it, if their jumps are judged in relation to their body size. A few tree-living kinds can travel 15 m or so, about 100 times their body length, by gliding through the air. Their toes have become very long and the web of skin between them so big that each foot is like a small parachute.

The frog's leap is not merely a way of getting from one place to another. It is also a good method of escaping from an enemy. As frogs and toads, with their soft-skinned bodies, are much sought after as food, they need all the defences they can muster. Many rely on camouflage, blending in with their surroundings. Some match the green of the glossy leaves on which they sit. Others, camouflaged with blotches of brown and grey, are almost invisible crouching among the leaf litter on the forest floor.

An Australian tree frog

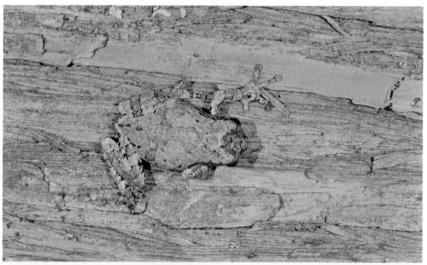

Camouflaged amphibians
The chorus frog (*left*) from North America, the toad from the jungle floor of South America (*below left*) and the natterjack toad from Europe (*below*) have bodies that not only match the colour of their backgrounds but are boldly patterned so that their tell-tale shapes are disguised.

The invasion of the land

But some frogs and toads defend themselves in a more active way. The common European toad, when it meets a snake, blows up its body to such a size that most snakes leave it alone. When alarmed, the firebellied toad throws itself on its back, so showing its yellow and black underside as a warning. This is not entirely a bluff. All amphibians have glands in their skin which produces slime to help to keep it moist. The firebelly's glands also produce a bitter-tasting poison. In central and South America at least 20 kinds of frogs have developed this defence still further. The poison they produce in their skins is so strong that it can kill a bird or a monkey. They are brightly coloured to warn off their attackers.

The defences of frogs
Many frogs, like these two from South America (*above and below right*), have poison in their skins and warn attackers of that fact with bright colours. The European toad (*right*), when meeting a snake, reacts by rearing up and taking in air so that it appears to be very big. The red-eyed frog from South America (*below left*) looks green when crouching on a leaf but, if disturbed, it jumps and suddenly shows the brilliant colours on the inner side of its legs.

A firebellied toad (*left*)

Arrow poison frogs
The poison in the skin of several
South American frogs (*above,
below, below left and bottom*) is so
powerful that the jungle Indians use
it on the tips of their arrows.

The invasion of the land

From the beginning, amphibians were hunters, preying on worms, insects and other animals. Today, some amphibians are still quite impressive hunters. The horned toad of South America has a gape so big that it can easily swallow nestling birds and young mice. But no amphibian is really nimble, and in order to catch their prey they rely not on speed, but on their tongues.

The amphibian was the first animal which could stick out its tongue. Because the tongue is attached to the front of the mouth, frogs and toads can stick it out much further than we can, simply by flicking it forward. Its end is both sticky and muscular so that the toad can use it first to grasp a worm or a slug and then to carry it back to the mouth.

Many amphibians have teeth as their ancestors had, but these are used for defence or as a way of gripping the prey. They cannot break up the food into easily swallowed pieces. Amphibians cannot chew, so they have to swallow their prey whole. The tongue helps by producing a lot of mucus, or slime, which helps the food slip down

A European tree frog catching a bluebottle

the throat. The tongue also pushes the food back along the floor of the mouth. So, it seems, do the eyes. All frogs and toads blink when they swallow. Their eye sockets have no bony floor, so when they blink, the eyeballs are drawn into the skull. This makes a bulge in the roof of the mouth which squeezes the lump of food to the back of the throat.

The amphibians' eyes work just as well out of water as in it. A fish's eye is kept clean because it is permanently washed as it swims. The amphibian, on land, has to have another method. It blinks. Frogs and toads have eardrums with which to detect sound in the air. They also have voices. Indeed, they are most impressive singers. Many frogs amplify the sound of their voices with huge swelling throats or sacs bulging from the corner of the jaws. A group of frogs, calling in a tropical swamp, can create such a noise that you have to shout to make yourself heard. Such noises as these must have been the first loud animal calls ever to sound on land, for before then there had only been the chirps and whirrs of insects.

A European marsh frog calling

A New Guinea tree frog calling

The invasion of the land

The amphibians' chorus, rising from a pool or a swamp, is a mating call. Most amphibians still mate in water. The female lays her eggs and the male, while grasping her, releases his sperm which swim to the eggs and fertilize them in the water. Then the adults return to land and leave the eggs behind. The number of eggs laid is enormous. A female toad may lay 20,000 eggs each season – perhaps a quarter of a million in her lifetime. Out of all these, only two have to live to maturity to keep the population the same.

The development of the spawn of a European frog

The adults mate, the male clasping the female.

10 days: the tadpoles wriggle out of the jelly.

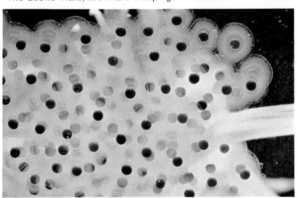

Spawn, a few hours after being laid.

13 days: newly emerged tadpoles with external gills.

9 days: the eggs grow within the jelly.

4–5 weeks: the tadpoles now eat meat – a worm.

7 weeks: the hind legs have just appeared.

Not all tadpoles develop at the same rate.

8 weeks: the forelegs are developing in the gill cavity.

13 weeks: the tail begins to dwindle.

9 weeks: the hind legs are growing.

16 weeks: the froglets have left the water.

11 weeks: all four legs have grown.

The young adult frog.

The invasion of the land

A female Pipa toad with eggs
embedded in her back

A male arrow poison frog carrying
tadpoles on his back

Some frogs have developed a different way of making sure enough of their young survive. They lay only a few eggs but they look after them very carefully. The Pipa toad is a grotesque creature with a flattened body and a squashed-looking head. After mating, the male gathers up the eggs with his webbed feet and gently spreads them over the female's back. And there they stick. The skin beneath them begins to swell and soon the eggs appear to be embedded in it. A thin membrane rapidly grows over them. Within 30 hours, the eggs have disappeared from sight and the skin of the female's back is smooth once more. Beneath the skin, the eggs develop. After a fortnight the whole of the female's back is rippling with the movements of the tadpoles beneath the skin. Then, after 24 days, the young break holes in the skin and swim away to seek safe hiding places.

When the first amphibians appeared, there was one safe place for their eggs and young – the land. No other animals were there to steal eggs and gulp the tadpoles as they did in the water. If the amphibians could lay their eggs out of water, their young would have better chances of survival. But there were problems. How could the eggs be kept from drying out and how could tadpoles develop out of water? Breeding on land is not so safe today for the amphibians no longer have it to themselves. There are reptiles, birds and even mammals that will eat amphibians' eggs and tadpoles if they can. Nonetheless, even today, many frogs and toads still breed on land.

A male midwife toad carrying
spawn on his legs

The European midwife toad spends most of its life in holes not far
from water. It mates on land. As the eggs are laid, the male fertilizes
them with his sperm. A quarter of an hour later, he begins to take up
the strings of eggs, twining them around his hind legs. For the next
few weeks, he hobbles about with them wherever he goes.
Eventually, when the eggs are about to hatch, he hops down to the
edge of the pool. He dips his legs with the eggs attached to them into
the water and stays there until all the tadpoles hatch. Then he returns
to his hole.

In Africa, there are frogs that manage to breed on the branches of
trees. They choose one that overhangs water. They mate and the
female produces a liquid from her vent which she beats into a foam
with her legs. In this she lays the eggs. The eggs hatch and the young
tadpoles develop within the foam. Eventually they fall into the water
below and swim away.

Other frogs produce young that go through the tadpole stage
without breaking out of the skin of the egg. As they cannot feed, as
free-swimming tadpoles can, they have to nourish themselves
entirely from the yolk. The female must therefore lay very yolky
eggs. Because of this, she can produce only a few. The whistling frog
from the Caribbean lays only a dozen or so, which she places on the
ground. Development is very rapid and within 20 days each egg
contains a tiny froglet. It pierces the skin of the egg and so hatches
without having been in water at all.

An African tree frog with its foam
nest

The invasion of the land

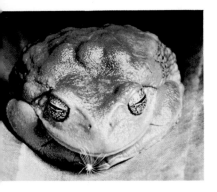

A female Gastrotheca frog
The pouch beneath the skin of her back is full of her young.

An Australian water-holding frog in its burrow

The most complicated ways of breeding are those in which the eggs and the developing young are kept moist actually inside the body of the parent. The female of one South American frog, Gastrotheca, has a pouch on her back with a slit-shaped entrance. As the eggs are laid and fertilized, she raises her rear with her hind legs so that the eggs roll down her back into the pouch. There they develop and hatch. Eventually the female widens the opening with her hind foot and the fully developed young clamber out.

The strangest of all these techniques is that practised by Rhinoderma, a tiny frog in southern Chile. The females lay their eggs on the moist ground, and the males sit in groups around them on guard. As soon as the developing eggs begin to move within their globes of jelly, the males lean forward and appear to eat them. Instead of swallowing them, however, the eggs are taken into the vocal sac which is unusually large and goes right down the underside of the male's body. There they develop into tadpoles. Then one day the male gulps once or twice, suddenly yawns and a fully formed froglet leaps out of his mouth.

So by these and many more complicated ways, frogs and toads have become less dependent on water for mating and for rearing young. Their skins, which cannot keep in moisture, force them to live somewhere moist to avoid drying out. But one or two kinds have even found a way around this.

There could scarcely be a less promising place for an amphibian to live than the desert of central Australia where several years may pass without any rain falling. And yet a few kinds of frogs manage to live even here. The water-holding frog, Cyclorana, appears above ground only during the brief rainstorms. Water then may lie on the rocks of the desert for several days, even a week or so. With frantic speed, the frogs feast on the great number of insects that have also hatched with the rain. And they mate, laying their eggs in the shallow pools. The eggs hatch and the tadpoles develop extremely swiftly.

As the rain water soaks away and the desert once again dries, the frogs absorb water through their skins until they are bloated and almost round. Then they dig deep into the soft sand and make a small chamber. Here they produce a membrane from their skins so that they look like plastic-wrapped fruit from a supermarket. This prevents water from evaporating from the skin. The frog can remain like this, moving hardly at all, for at least two years – much like its distant cousin, the lungfish.

Nonetheless, even this frog is dependent upon rains arriving at some time and it is only active when the desert is wet. To survive, remain active and breed in areas where there is little or no rain and no open water at all, a creature must have both a watertight skin and a watertight egg. The development of those two characteristics was the next great breakthrough. It brought to an end the era of amphibians and it was introduced by the next great group of animals to appear, the reptiles.

7 · A watertight skin

If there is one place on earth where the reptiles still rule, it must be in the Galapagos Islands in the Pacific. There, rocks are still covered with herds of lizards and giant tortoises lumber through the cactus. The Galapagos are made of volcanic lava and lie on the equator, roasting in the sun. An amphibian here would be shrivelled by the heat and killed within minutes. But the iguanas flourish. They can do so because, unlike amphibians, their skins are watertight.

There are two kinds of iguanas on the islands – the land iguanas which live in the scrub and marine iguanas that swarm on the bare lava by the coast. Basking in the sun, for them, is a necessary activity. The working of any animal's body is greatly affected by heat. The higher the temperature, the more energy it can produce. Neither the reptiles nor the amphibians can make their own heat. Instead, they draw it from their surroundings. As amphibians cannot expose themselves directly to the sun, because they would dry out, they remain cold and therefore sluggish. But the reptiles have no such problems.

The marine iguanas follow a daily routine that keeps their bodies at the right temperature. At dawn they lie sideways to the sun, absorbing as much heat as possible. As they grow warmer, they turn to face the sun so the rays strike only their chests. As the sun climbs

The marine iguanas of the Galapagos
These reptiles spend much of the day basking in the sun (*above*). In some places, they assemble in great herds (*bottom left*), young and adults mixed together (*below*). Most are grey or black but those on Hood Island (*bottom right*) are quite brightly coloured.

Marine iguanas at sea
They swim by beating their tails
(*above*) and can dive below the
surface to graze on seaweed (*top*).

higher and higher, they run the risk of overheating. Although reptile skin is watertight it does not have sweat glands, so the iguanas cannot cool themselves by sweating. To cool down they lift their bodies off the hot lava and try to hide in the shade or in cracks in the rocks. The iguanas are vegetarians. No edible plants grow on the lava, but in the sea there are thick pastures of green algae. So, during the middle of the day when their blood is almost as hot as they can stand and they are in danger of sunstroke, they risk a swim. They plunge into the surf, swimming strongly, beating their tails like giant newts. Some cling to the rocks near the sea's edge, gnawing the seaweed. Others dive to browse on the sea bottom.

But they cannot stay in the cold water for very long. After a few minutes the temperature of their bodies has dropped some 10°C and they have to return to land. Back on the rocks, they lie with all four legs outstretched. Not until their bodies warm up again will they be able to digest their meal. In the late afternoon, the risk of chilling returns and they gather once more on the ridges to absorb the last rays of the setting sun.

In this way, the iguanas manage to keep their bodies very close to 37°C – almost exactly the temperature of the human body. Clearly the label 'cold-blooded', so often applied to reptiles, is a very misleading one.

There are many advantages to producing one's heat from within the body as birds and mammals do. Such animals can remain active at night when the warming sun has disappeared and live in cold parts of the world where no reptile can survive. But the price paid for such privileges is very high. Something like 80% of the energy in our food goes towards maintaining our body temperature at a constant level. Reptiles, by taking their heat directly from the sun, can survive on 10% of the nourishment that a mammal of similar size needs. As a result, reptiles can live in deserts where a mammal would starve, and the marine iguanas flourish on quantities of vegetation that would not keep a rabbit alive.

Reptiles not only survive in waterless places, they manage to breed there too. So their eggs must be watertight like their bodies. As the egg is being laid, a gland inside the female deposits a parchment-like shell around the egg. Clearly, however, if this shell is thick enough to prevent the egg from drying out, then it will prevent sperm getting in. Fertilization must, therefore, take place within the female's body before the shell is laid. To deal with this problem the male is equipped with an organ, called a penis, to deposit sperm inside the female.

Only one reptile today lacks a penis, a strange lizard-like creature, the tuatara, that lives in a few small islands in New Zealand. The tuatara achieves internal fertilization in the same way as some salamanders and frogs. When the pair come together, their sexual openings are pressed closely together so that sperm from the male swims into the female's opening. The tuatara resembles the amphibians in another way. It remains active at temperatures below

7°C, which is much lower than any lizard or snake could stand for long. It seems, therefore, to be a very primitive kind of reptile. Bones of an almost identical creature have been found in rocks 200 million years old.

The four-legged, tough-skinned, egg-laying reptiles soon after they first developed became adapted to life in all parts of the world except in polar regions. Some, the ichthyosaurs and plesiosaurs, became water-living with their legs turned into paddles. Others grew a long finger on each foreleg which supported sail-like flaps of leathery skin, and took to the air as pterosaurs. And the land was ruled by the dinosaurs.

Some dinosaurs were no bigger than a chicken. Others were the biggest land-living creatures the world has ever seen. Why did some dinosaurs grow to such a great size? There are at least two possible reasons. The teeth of some of the biggest, such as Apatosaurus (which used to be called Brontosaurus and was some 25 m long and may have been 30 tonnes in weight), show that they were vegetarians. The teeth were not very effective and the pulping of the food was done in the dinosaur's stomach by digestive juices. Because this took a long time, the dinosaur's stomach had to be huge to store the food while it was being digested. A huge stomach requires a huge body to carry it. Meat-eating dinosaurs, like Tyrannosaurus, had, in turn, to be large to be able to prey on the giant plant-eaters.

The second advantage of great size to the dinosaurs was connected with temperature control. The bigger a body, the longer it keeps its heat. Temperature control may also explain the unusual body form of some types of dinosaurs. The Stegosaurus carried along its back a line of diamond-shaped plates. It was once thought that these were a kind of armour, but close examination has shown that each plate was covered with skin thick with blood vessels. The animal may have controlled its temperature in the same way as the marine iguanas do today. If it stood sideways to the sun, its blood would heat very quickly as it flowed over the plates. If it faced the sun – and particularly if there was any kind of breeze – the plates would become cooling radiators.

Procompsognathus
Length: 90cm ◁

Scelidosaurus △
Length: 4m

Dilophosaurus
Length: 6m ◁

Kentros
Length:

Heterodontosaurus ◁
Length: 90cm

Ceratosaurus △
Length: 6m

Coelophysis ◁
Length: 3m

Diplodocus △
Length: 26m

Megalosaurus
Length: 6-7m ▽

Ornitholestes ▷
Length: 1.5m

Plateosaurus △
Length: 6m

Camptosaurus △
Length: 5m

Compsognathus △
Length: 60cm

195 million years ago

THE DINOSAUR FAMILY

The first fossils of dinosaurs to be discovered were found in the rocks of southern England. It was these that were given the name dinosaur meaning 'terrible lizard'. Since then many specimens have been discovered all over the world. The most spectacular ones have been unearthed in the United States.

These reptiles ruled the earth for over 100 million years. During this vast time, several hundred different species appeared, flourished and vanished, to be succeeded by others. In this picture, a few of them have been drawn to the same scale and arranged in a procession, starting on the left with the

Brachiosaurus
▽ Length: 26m

Scolosaurus
Length: 6m ▽

Hypsilophodon △
Length: 2m

Polacanthus
▽ Length: 4m

Pachycephalosaurus
Length: 6-8m
◁

Ornithomimus
Length: 4m

◁ Camarasaurus
Length: 18m

Parasaurolophus
Length: 10m
◁

Corythrosaurus
Length: 9m ▷

Psittacosaurus
Length: 2m

Deinonychus
Length: 3m

Tyrannosaurus
Length: 13m
◁

Protoceratops
Length: 2m
▷

◁ Monoclonius
Length: 6m

Styracosaurus
Length: 6m
▽

Spinosaurus
Length: 11m △

million years ago   **64 million years ago △**

earliest, which lived some 225 million years ago, and ending with the last on the right which suddenly disappeared 64 million years ago. Not all of them were monsters. Some were delicate bird-like creatures such as the early Procompsognathus, which walked on its hind legs and preyed on other smaller creatures. It was about 30 cm high at the hips. The giants, like Diplodocus, Brachiosaurus and Camarasaurus, were all vegetarians. The biggest dinosaurs weighed about 75 tonnes. Towards the end of the dinosaurs' time, the flesh-eating species increased in size. The most formidable of these was Tyrannosaurus.

A watertight skin

A dinosaur's trail
About 120 million years ago a flesh-eating dinosaur walked on its hind legs across a mud flat in what is now Texas. The mud turned to stone, preserving the three-toed footprints in excellent detail.

The bones of many of the smaller dinosaurs show that they were able to move very swiftly. To do this their blood temperature must have been quite high. It may be that they were able to produce heat within their bodies. What we do not know is whether they were able to maintain a steady body temperature. To do that all warm-blooded animals have some kind of heat insulation above or just below their skins – hair, fat or feathers. No reptile skin has such insulation today, nor is there any evidence that the dinosaurs ever had any.

There have been many suggestions as to what brought the dinosaurs to their end. One is that there was some kind of worldwide catastrophe. This is unlikely because it was only the dinosaurs that disappeared, not all animals – or even all reptiles. Another theory suggests that the mammals began to compete with the dinosaurs for food and because they were more intelligent they brought an end to the dinosaurs. But fossil records show that although mammals had been in existence for many millions of years before the dinosaurs disappeared, they were very small creatures about the size of a shrew. It is just possible that such creatures could have preyed on dinosaur eggs, but it seems unlikely that they could have destroyed a single species, let alone all the dinosaurs.

Fossil plants, however, provide a more convincing explanation. They suddenly change their character in a way which suggests a change in climate. It seems that about 63 million years ago, at the time the dinosaurs disappeared, the climate on earth got colder. This may very well have killed the dinosaurs. While it is true that a big body retains heat for a long time, it is also true that it takes a very long time to regain heat once it has been lost. Even if some of the dinosaurs could produce their own body heat, a few bitterly cold nights could have drained a big dinosaur of its heat beyond all recovery. With its body badly chilled, it would not have had enough energy to search for food. So a steady cooling of the climate may have killed off the large plant-eating dinosaurs. With them would go the meat-eaters that hunted them. The pterosaurs, huddled on their cliffs, would not have been able to survive either.

There are two ways to escape the cold which are used by various reptiles alive today. One is to find a crack in rocks or to bury itself so that it is beyond the reach of the worst frosts. But that is only possible if the reptile is small. Apatosaurus or Tyrannosaurus had no chance of doing so. The other is to take to the water. Since water retains heat much longer than air, the effects of a sudden cold spell are less. A long cold season can be avoided by swimming to warmer areas. This method could be used by big creatures if they could swim. The three main types of reptile that survive today from the period of the dinosaurs – the crocodiles, the lizards, and the tortoises and turtles – can either creep into holes in the ground or swim.

Fossil crocodiles appear in the rocks at about the same time as dinosaurs. Their direct descendants are today the largest of all living reptiles. Males of the huge sea-going species that live in southeast Asia grow to be over 6 m long.

Crocodiles hatching
These babies can give a sharp bite even before they are completely out of their shells.

The Nile crocodile spends most of its days basking on sandbanks, keeping an even body temperature in much the same way as the Galapagos iguanas, though its larger size makes it less sensitive to small temperature changes. It has a special way of cooling itself. It opens its mouth so that air cools the soft skin inside. At night, it moves down into the waters of the river to stay warm. The social lives of crocodiles are quite complex. The male establishes a breeding territory, patrolling a patch of water not far from a beach. He bellows and fights any other males that come too close. Courtship takes place in the water. As the female approaches, the male becomes greatly excited. He roars, lashes his tail and claps his huge jaws in frenzy. Actual mating lasts only a couple of minutes as the male clasps the female with his jaws and their tails intertwine.

A Nile crocodile

The female digs a hole in the bank above the waterline. She lays at night, producing about 40 eggs in several batches. The holes are never made in places that are exposed to full sunshine throughout the day. Other species go to even greater lengths to ensure that their eggs remain at an even temperature. The saltwater crocodile builds a mound of vegetation as a nest and sprays urine over it when it gets too hot.

A crocodile carrying its young

A radiated tortoise from Madagascar

When the eggs of the Nile crocodile are close to hatching, the young within begin to make piping calls. These are so loud that they can be heard, through shell and sand, from several metres away. The female begins to scrape away the sand covering the eggs. As the young struggle up through the sand, she picks them up with her jaws, using her huge teeth gently and delicately. She has a special pouch in the bottom of her mouth where she can hold half a dozen babies. When she has collected such a number, she carries them down to the water. Then she swims away, with her jaws half-closed and the young peering through her teeth. The male helps and within a short time the young have been moved to a special nursery area in the swamp. Here they remain for a couple of months, hiding in small holes in the bank and hunting for frogs and fish while their parents keep guard. It is possible that the dinosaurs had similarly complicated forms of courtship and parental behaviour.

The tortoises have an ancestry just as ancient as the crocodiles. They have invested in defence. They enlarged their scales into horny plates and reinforced them from below with bone. So their bodies became enclosed in a box into which they could withdraw their head and legs to protect themselves. It is the most effective armour developed by any vertebrate.

One group of them took to the water and became the turtles. It was easier for such heavy creatures to swim than to move on land. But the shelled eggs that had enabled their ancestors to leave the water were useless in it. So the female turtle has to return to land to lay her eggs just like her relations.

The green turtle
This reptile spends most of its life at sea (*top left*) but the female has to come ashore to lay her eggs (*below left*). She digs a pit in the sand above high-tide mark (*top right*) and in the bottom she lays several dozen soft-shelled eggs.

Green turtle hatchlings
The young struggle unaided from the papery shells of their eggs (*left*), haul themselves up through the sand with their flippers, and then scuttle down the beach to the sea (*bottom*).

A watertight skin

The third group of survivors, the lizards, are very much more numerous than either the crocodiles or the turtles. There are now many different families – iguanas, chameleons, skinks, monitors and several others. They have all protected their watertight skins by developing their scales. Scales, like our own fingernails, are made of a dead horny material and gradually wear away. The lizards have to replace them often several times a year. A new set grows beneath the old which are then cast off. Scales are more than just protection. They can be used in display. Marine iguanas have a crest of long ones along their spines so that the males look big and impressive. Some chameleons have grown their head scales into horns – single, double, triple or even quadruple.

Throughout their history the lizards, like the salamanders of America, have had a tendency to lose their legs. Several skinks today represent different stages of the process. Australian ones, like the blue-tongue or the shingleback, have tiny legs scarcely strong enough to carry their bodies. Another lizard, the European slow-worm, has no legs at all, although it still has traces of the bones inside its body. It was this tendency that, 100 million years ago, led to the appearance of the snakes.

Geckos
These small lizards have very special feet. The scales of their toes (*above*) have tiny hooks on them that enable their owners to cling to walls and run upside-down over ceilings. The flying gecko (*above right*) also has flaps of skin on its flanks and between its toes so that it can make gliding jumps. The tokay gecko (*below left*) gets its name from the sound of its call. Like all lizards, geckos periodically shed their skins (*below right*).

The scales of lizards

Scales can do more than protect their owners' bodies against wear and tear. The sungazer lizard of Africa (*left*) has scales so long and spiky that they give it good protection against creatures that might eat it. The Gila monster (*bottom*) has a poisonous bite and its bright pink scales may serve as warning colours. The tiny thorny devil from Australia (*top*) uses its scales in a particularly odd way. At night in the desert, the dew condenses on them. The moisture is then drawn down minute grooves in the scales to its mouth.

A watertight skin

Chameleons

There are about 80 different kinds of chameleons. The common chameleon (*above*) is found around the Mediterranean coast including southern Spain. Most of the rest live in Madagascar, like the white striped one (*middle left*), or in Africa like the three-horned one (*below*). The female three-horned lacks horns and gives birth to live young (*top right*). When threatened, chameleons hiss alarmingly (*middle right*). Most have very long tongues which they can shoot out to catch insects (*bottom right*).

A European slow-worm (*below*)
It is neither a worm nor a snake, but a lizard that has lost its legs.

The skinks
This, the biggest of the lizard families, has 800 different kinds in it. They are found all over the warmer parts of the world. The shingleback (*top left*) and the blue-tongued skink (*below right*) live in Australia. The blue-tailed skink (*left*) is found in eastern Australia and many Pacific islands.

A watertight skin

No one doubts that the snakes once had legs. Indeed, pythons and boas still have traces of hipbones inside and two spurs on the outside. They may have lost their legs because they took to burrowing underground. The fact that they have no eardrums either supports this idea, for burrowing animals tend to lose their hearing since it is of little value underground. Without legs, the snakes had to develop new means of getting about. The usual method is to flex the side muscles alternately so that the body is drawn up into a series of S-shaped curves. As the contractions travel in waves down the body, the flanks are pressed against stones or plant stems and the snake pushes itself forward. In short, it wriggles. If it is put on a surface completely free of any roughness, this cannot work and the snake writhes helplessly.

If the ancestral snakes did indeed spend a period below ground, their prey is likely to have been invertebrates such as worms and termites and perhaps the early shrew-like mammals. When they came above ground, their scope became very much greater. A few boas and pythons now grow to such a length that they can tackle creatures as big as goats and antelope. Having seized their prey with

Snakes that kill by squeezing
A python first seizes its prey with its jaws. Then it swiftly wraps its coils around it. The reticulate python (*right*) has captured a rat. The Indian python (*bottom right*), one of the biggest of all snakes, is eating a deer, having unhinged its lower jaw in order to do so. The green tree python from New Guinea (*bottom left*) catches young birds and lizards and the black-headed python from Australia (*above*) eats other snakes.

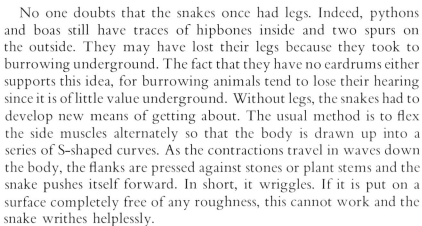

their mouths, they swiftly coil themselves around it and then kill it by tightening their coils so that their victim cannot breathe. It dies by suffocation rather than by crushing.

The more advanced snakes kill, not by squeezing their prey to death, but by poison. The back-fanged snakes deliver the poison by means of specially adapted teeth near the back of the upper jaw. The poison glands lie above these teeth and the poison trickles down a groove in the tooth. Once the prey has been bitten, the back-fanged snake holds its grip and chews, rocking its jaw from side to side until the fangs are at last driven into the victim's flesh carrying their poison with them.

Other snakes have still more refined ways of killing. Their fangs are placed at the front of the upper jaw and have a hollow passage through which the poison flows. Cobras, mambas and sea-snakes have short fangs, but those of vipers are so long that they have to be kept hinged back, lying flat along the roof of the mouth. When the snake strikes, its mouth opens wide and the fangs are brought down and forward so that they will stab the victim. As they pierce the flesh, the poison is injected down them.

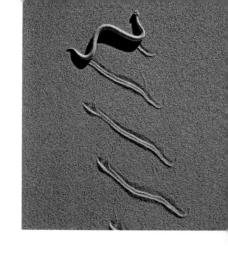

Venomous snakes
The most poisonous snakes have long fangs at the front of the mouth like the rattlesnake *(left)*. They can move very swiftly when necessary. The sidewinder *(above)* scuttles along with a strange sideways motion. The black cobra uses a straightforward wriggle *(bottom)*. They usually favour mammals as prey. The rhinoceros viper *(below)* has caught a rat.

A watertight skin

The snakes were the last of the great reptile groups to appear and the most advanced of them are the pit vipers. The rattlesnakes of Mexico and the southwest of the United States belong to this group. Like many other snakes, and some amphibians and fish before them, the rattlesnakes protect their eggs by keeping them inside the body. The shell becomes a thin membrane so that the developing young not only feed on the yolk but draw nourishment from their mother's blood while inside her body. It is a process similar to the placenta that is used by the mammals. Nor does the female rattler abandon her young once they are born. She actively guards them, warning off enemies with the sound of her rattle.

A rattlesnake hunts mostly at night with the aid of a detector no other animal possesses. Between the nostril and the eye is the pit which gives the group of snakes its name. It reacts to heat and is so sensitive that it detects a rise of $1/300°C$. What is more, it helps the snake to identify the direction where the heat comes from. So, with the aid of its pits, the rattlesnake in total darkness is able to find a small ground squirrel crouching motionless half a metre away. The snake slides towards it in near-silence. Once within range it strikes, shooting its head forward at a speed of 3 m a second. Then its huge fangs inject its victim with deadly poison. It is one of the most efficient killers in the animal world.

The rattlesnake does not need much food because, like all reptiles, it can absorb the sun's energy directly. A dozen or so meals a year are quite enough for it. Curled up among the stones and cactus of the Mexican desert, it is the master of its environment and fears nothing.

The reptiles, because of their watertight skins and eggs, were the first vertebrates to colonize the desert. In some places, some of them still own it.

A rattlesnake
The snake's rattle (*top*) is a clump of hollow scales at the end of its tail which makes a rattling noise when the snake quivers its tail. It senses the presence of its prey (*right*) by tasting the air with its tongue and detecting the heat of its prey's body by means of a pair of pits, one each side of its head midway between and below the nostril and the eye. The rattler strikes (*above*) by lunging forward with its jaws open and its fangs unsheathed.

8. Lords of the air

A body feather from an owl

The feather is an extraordinary object. It is made of the same horny material that forms a reptile's scales and our own nails. A central shaft carries on either side about 100 tiny filaments. Each filament is again fringed with about 100 smaller filaments. In downy feathers this structure produces an air-trapping fluffiness and so gives superb insulation. In flight feathers, the filaments hook onto one another so that they form a continuous surface which has great strength. Almost all the characteristics that distinguish birds from other animals can be traced to these two benefits brought by feathers. Indeed, the very possession of a feather is enough to define a creature as a bird.

In 1860, in Solnhofen in Germany, the delicate outline of a single fossil feather was found in a slab of limestone. It caused a sensation, because these rocks dated from the days of the dinosaurs, long before birds were then thought to exist.

A tail feather from a peacock

To what kind of bird had it belonged? A year later, searchers discovered the fossilized skeleton of a feathered creature the size of a pigeon. Scientists called it Archaeopteryx, meaning 'ancient wing'. It lay sprawling on the rock with its wings outstretched, and all around it, the clear print of its feathers. It was very different from any living bird. It had a long bony tail with feathers sprouting on either side of it and it had claws, not only on its feet but on the three toes of its feathered forelimbs. Later, another example was found complete with its skull, which showed that the creature had not a beak like a modern bird, but a jaw with teeth.

Archaeopteryx was as much a reptile as a bird. Its feathers seem to have developed from the scales of its reptilian ancestors. Undoubtedly they insulated it very well, so it would have been able to maintain a high body temperature, something which was very difficult for its dinosaur cousins to do. With a warm body, Archaeopteryx must have been able to move swiftly even during the cool hours of the day.

But why did it have wing feathers? The size and shape of its breastbone show that its wing muscles were very small – so small that it could not flap its wings powerfully enough to take off into the air from the ground. What, then, did it use its wings for? One explanation is that they enabled it to glide from branch to branch, just as gliding lizards do today. Archaeopteryx was certainly able to

climb in trees. One of its four toes pointed backwards, giving it a powerful grasp. And the claws on the front of its feathered forewings could have helped it to cling to branches.

One living bird, the hoatzin, shows how it might have used these claws. The hoatzin is a curious heavily-built bird, the size of a chicken, that lives in the swamps of Guyana and Venezuela. Its nest is a roughly built platform of twigs, built above water, often in mangroves. When the young first hatch they are naked and very active. They have two little claws on the front edge of each wing with which they cling to twigs. In these naked young birds you can see a hint of the way Archaeopteryx may have moved through the branches. The adult hoatzins are poor flyers, but they are unquestionably very much better than Archaeopteryx ever was. Like all modern birds they have a skeleton that has become greatly modified for flight.

It is very important for every flyer to keep its weight to a minimum. Archaeopteryx's bones were solid, like a reptile's. Those of modern birds are paper-thin or hollow. Instead of Archaeopteryx's heavy bony tail, today's birds have fans of stout feathers as tails. Instead of jawbones armed with teeth, they have light horny beaks. But without teeth even the best beak cannot chew and most birds still need to break up their food in order to digest it. They do that with a special compartment of the stomach, the gizzard.

The first bird
The oldest known feathered creature is Archaeopteryx. The first sign of its existence was a single fossilized feather (*opposite page below*) found in 1860 in limestone laid down about 140 million years ago. A year after, a skeleton was found (*opposite page above*). Its tail has a long bony rod running down it as a reptile's tail has, but the marks of feathers sprouting from either side can clearly be seen. So too can the spread feathers on its forelimbs. Other fossils found later showed clearly that three of the toes on each forelimb had claws on them. Perhaps Archaeopteryx used them to help it clamber through the branches as young hoatzin birds (*above*) do today.

Lords of the air

Beaks have developed into different shapes to suit the diets of their owners. The sword-billed hummingbird has a long thin beak, four times the length of its body to suck nectar from flowers. The macaw has a hooked nutcracker so it can split the hardest nuts. The woodpecker uses its beak like a drill to excavate wood-boring insects. The flamingo's crooked beak has a fine sieve with which it traps tiny crustaceans. The list of bill shapes is nearly endless.

Different foods – different beaks
The bald eagle rips carcasses apart (*top right*); the shoebill stork (*middle left*) catches lungfish and catfish; the lovebird (*middle right*) cracks seeds; the pelican (*bottom right*) nets fish in its baggy bill; and the green woodpecker (*below*) drills holes in wood to find insects.

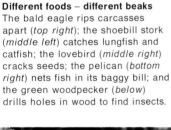

Different foods – different beaks
The skimmer (*above*) flies over water with its beak open so that the lower half of it just cuts the water surface. When it touches a fish, the beak snaps shut. The spoonbill (*left*) sieves through the ooze in lake shallows by swinging its bill from side to side. The avocet (*below*) collects small insect larvae and shrimps by moving its head in a similar way and using its slim beak like forceps.

Feathers for warmth
Chinstrap penguins breed on the Antarctic continent as well as on many of the sub-Antarctic islands. Their feathers grow so densely that they form coats which keep the birds warm, not only as they swim in the near-freezing seas, but when they stand on ice floes and even during blizzards.

Most of the foods birds choose – fish, nuts, nectar, insect larvae, fruit – are rich in energy. Birds need these high-energy foods because flying is an extremely energetic business. To ensure that energy is not wasted in the form of heat, insulation is of the greatest importance. As insulators, feathers are even more efficient than fur. Only a bird – the penguin – can survive on the Antarctic icecap in winter, the coldest place on earth.

Feathers are regularly moulted and renewed, usually once a year. Even so they need constant care. Their owners wash them in water and ruffle them in dust. Most birds have an oil gland in the skin near the base of the tail. The bird squeezes oil from it with its beak and spreads it on its feathers so that they are kept water-repellent. Some birds, including herons, parrots and toucans, lack the gland. They condition their feathers with a fine dust that is produced from a special clump of feathers.

Birds also need to pick off fleas and lice from their skins. Jays, starlings and jackdaws and several other species get rid of such parasites by encouraging other insects to crawl over their skins. They will squat on an ant nest with feathers ruffled, so that the disturbed ants swarm all over them. All this toiletry takes up a great deal of a bird's non-flying time, but its reward comes when it takes to the air.

Feather care
All flying birds must spend a lot of time preening to keep their feathers in good order, as these are doing – a snowy egret (*top left*), a snake bird (*bottom left*), a flamingo (*above*) and a king vulture (*below*).

Different wing shapes – different flight

The short broad wings of a hummingbird (*below*) beat so fast that they enable the bird to hover. The brown pelican (*above*) dives onto shoals of fish at sea and can pull back its wings to give it added speed to its dive.

Birds' wings have a much more complex job to do than the wings of an aeroplane. In addition to supporting the bird they must act as its engine, rowing it through the air. Even so the wings give the same kind of support in the air as those of an aeroplane. So if you know how different kinds of aircraft perform, you can make a good guess about how similarly shaped birds will fly.

Short stubby wings enable a tanager to swerve and dodge through the forest just as they helped the fighter planes of the Second World War to make tight turns in a dog-fight. More modern fighters reach greater speeds by sweeping back their wings while in flight, just as peregrines do when they go into a 130 km/h dive, stooping to a kill. Championship gliders have long thin wings so that they can soar gently for hours and an albatross, the largest of flying birds, with a similar wing shape and a span of 3 m, can patrol the ocean for hours in the same way without a single wing beat. Vultures and hawks circle at very slow flying speeds and they have the broad rectangular wings that slow-flying aircraft have. Humans have not been able to design wings that by themselves provide hovering flight but hummingbirds have such wings. By beating their wings as fast as 80 times a second, they can not only remain still in the air but even fly backwards.

Different wing shapes – different flight

The barn owl (*above*) has soft edges and tips to its wing feathers so that it can fly silently as it searches for its prey. The Andean condor (*top left*) has long wide wings with slots between the feathers at the ends that can be opened and closed. These wings enable it to circle in the rising currents of warm air that are found over land and glide for hours without a wingbeat. The black-browed albatross (*below*) has long slim wings suited to gliding at high speed in the strong and steady winds that blow over seas. The robin (*bottom left*) has short wide wings with slots that enable it to get a quick take-off and dodge and dive through branches and undergrowth.

Lords of the air

The greatest bird traveller
The Arctic tern (*right*) flies from the
Arctic to the Antarctic and back
again every year.

The fastest bird flyer
The swept-back curved wings of the
swift give it great speed. One kind,
the spine-tailed swift of Asia, is
probably the fastest flying of all
birds.

No other creatures can fly as far as or as long as birds. The swift can fly up to 170 km/h and about 900 km a day. It even mates in mid-air. A female holds out her wings stiffly and a male comes from behind, settles on her back and the two glide together. They never land between breeding seasons so that they spend at least nine months of the year continuously on the wing. Many species of birds make long yearly journeys. The European stork travels every autumn to Africa and returns to Europe in the spring, navigating with such accuracy that the pair will come back to the same roof top year after year.

The greatest traveller of all is the Arctic tern. Some nest well north of the Arctic Circle. A chick hatching in northern Greenland during July will, within a few weeks, set off on an 18,000 km flight that takes it to its summer grounds not far from the South Pole. The following May, it will head north back to Greenland. So it experiences both the Antarctic and the Arctic summers when the sun scarcely dips below the horizon, and sees more daylight each year than any other creature. The energy spent in flying such distances is gigantic, but the advantages are clear. At each end of its route it can tap a rich food supply that exists for only half the year.

But how do the birds manage to find their way? There is no single answer – they have many methods. Many birds use geographical landmarks. They follow coastlines, valleys, and mountain passes. But all birds do not rely on such straightforward methods. The Arctic tern, for example, has to fly at least 3000 km across the Antarctic Ocean with no land to guide it. Some birds that fly at night navigate by the stars. We know this because on cloudy nights they tend to get lost and birds released in a planetarium steer by the artificial constellations even if they are twisted at an angle to the true ones outside. Day-flying birds may use the sun. Still others appear to be able to use the earth's magnetic field as a guide. So it seems that many migrating birds must carry in their brains the equivalent of a clock, a compass and a map.

The feathers that keep a bird warm and enable it to fly are used in yet a third way. They serve as banners with which to send messages. For most of their lives the majority of birds try to remain unseen and their feathers provide the colours and patterns for perfect camouflage. But each year, at the beginning of the breeding season, birds need to communicate with one another. As male meets male in territorial dispute over nesting sites, they raise their feather crests, thrust out their coloured chests and display their wing patterns in a long series of threats and arguments. These visual signals are usually accompanied by calls. Both kinds of signals carry the same three messages – a declaration of the species of the bird, a challenge to any male of the same species and an invitation to a female to join him.

Making clear the species of the sender is obviously important to prevent birds wasting their time in courting and mating with partners with whom they cannot produce fertile eggs. Sometimes this is done mostly by song, but usually it is by the plumage.

At the same time as identifying their species, individual birds must also declare their sex to one another. If male and female look alike, then a bird must use some other way to make its sex clear. Penguins have this problem and the male penguin has a charming way of solving it. He picks up a pebble in his bill, waddles over to a bird standing alone and lays it before it. If he gets an outraged peck, he knows he has made a dreadful mistake – this is another male. If his offering is ignored, then he has found a female who is not yet ready to breed or already has a mate. He picks up his rejected gift and moves on. But if the stranger receives the pebble with a deep bow then he has discovered his true mate. He bows back and the two stretch up their necks and trumpet in celebration.

Many species, however, have a small detail that indicates their sex like the moustache of a bearded tit, the black bib of a sparrow or the different coloured eye of a parrot. During courtship the owner of such a badge shows it off in front of the partner who lacks it.

Dancing birds
The male and female wandering albatross (*above*) dance together at the nest, stretching their wings, rattling their bills and calling. They remain mated for life. Great crested grebes (*below*) perform long complicated dances on water. Both male and female have special feather adornments on their heads which they display to one another. In peafowl (*top left*) only the peacock grows a magnificent tail for display at breeding time. The female, here walking in front of him, is plain. The male golden pheasant (*top right*) also develops special display plumage which he flaunts not only to impress females but also during disputes with other males as is shown here.

Feathers for display
The Emperor Bird of Paradise (*bottom*) sprouts plumes from beneath his wings. The Blue Bird of Paradise (*below*) hangs upside-down to display. The Parotia Bird of Paradise (*above*) spreads a black skirt of feathers as he dances. The biggest feathers of all are wing feathers grown by the male argus pheasant (*right*) for his display dance.

Some groups of birds have developed the sexual difference in plumage to an extraordinary degree. The males of pheasants, grouse and birds of paradise grow feathers of great size and sensational colour and become so obsessed with displaying their costumes that they do little else and will mate with several different females in a season. The females are drab and after mating, return to lay their eggs and care for their young entirely by themselves. The male continues strutting and pirouetting, awaiting his next female visitor.

The island of New Guinea contains some 40 different species of birds of paradise. All of them have the most magnificent plumes though these are of many different kinds. Only the males bear them, and after the breeding season ends, they shed them.

Their relatives, the bower birds, which also live in New Guinea have found a more economical way of displaying. They use sticks, stones, flowers, seeds and any brightly coloured objects they can find, provided that they are of a particular colour. The males build bowers which they decorate with such treasures. One species arranges twigs around a sapling to form a maypole which it decorates with pieces of lichen. Another builds a roofed grotto with two entrances in front of which he gathers flowers, mushrooms and berries, each neatly stacked in its own pile.

The male satin bower bird which lives in Australia is a dark glossy

blue. He builds an avenue of twigs. At one end, he assembles his collection. There may be feathers, berries, even pieces of plastic – only their colour matters. Most are a shade of blue that matches his shining feathers. One way you can bring a satin bird down to his bower is to add to his collection an object of a different colour, such as a white snail shell. He usually returns very quickly and removes the offensive object, picking it up with his bill and throwing it aside. The females are dull-looking creatures. If he succeeds in luring one to the bower, mating takes place close by or inside the bower.

The actual mechanics of mating used by birds seem clumsy. The male, with only few exceptions, has no penis. He mounts on the female's back, sometimes steadying himself by clinging onto her head feathers with his beak. She twists her tail to one side so that the two openings are brought together and the sperm is transferred to the female. But the female has to remain very still or the male topples off and only too often it seems that the mating is unsuccessful.

All birds lay eggs. This is the one characteristic inherited from their reptilian ancestors that no bird anywhere has abandoned. Perhaps this is because a large egg inside the body, let alone several, would be too heavy for a female to carry in flight throughout the weeks necessary for development. So as soon as the egg within her is fertilized, the female lays it.

Display without feathers
Bower birds are close relations of the birds of paradise, but instead of growing feathers for their display, they use objects they find, such as flowers, pebbles and berries. The males build small avenues or grottos in which to show off their collections. Each kind of bower bird has its own favourite colour. The satin bower bird (*above*) prefers blue objects to all others.

Woven nests
The Baya weaver (*below*) uses plant fibres to weave a long tube with its entrance at the bottom. The hermit hummingbird (*right*) suspends its nest from the end of a leaf. To prevent it tipping up when the bird lands on the rim, the bird hangs bits of earth beneath the nest with spider's web silk to act as a counterweight. The giant hummingbird (*bottom*) takes advantage of the defences of a cactus by weaving its nest among the cactus's spines.

But now the birds must pay the penalty for having developed the hot blood necessary for flight. Reptiles can bury their eggs in holes or under stones and then abandon them. Their eggs, like the adults themselves, need no more than the normal heat of their surroundings to survive and develop. But the developing chicks have hot blood like their parents and if they get chilled, they will die.

Birds therefore have to incubate or sit on their eggs. This can be very dangerous because in such a position they are open to attack from their enemies. If they leave the nest, their eggs and young are put at risk. Yet the nest has to be approachable so that the parents themselves can take turns in incubating and leave it to collect food for themselves and the young.

Some birds nest in places that other animals find impossible to reach. Only a bird could get to a ledge in the middle of a sea cliff. But there is danger even there. The risk of the egg rolling off is reduced by laying eggs that are pointed at one end and which, if they do roll, go around in a circle. But unless parents are watchful, gulls will come and pick holes in their eggs and eat them. Other birds use camouflage to protect their eggs. Plovers and birds that live on gravelly shores lay their eggs out in the open for no cover exists. Their eggs are coloured to match the gravel so it is extremely difficult to pick them out.

Most birds, however, safeguard their eggs and young by building some kind of protection. The woodpecker makes holes in trees. The kingfisher bores into river banks. The tailor bird in India sews together the leaves of a tree forming a cup within which the bird builds its nest. The weaver bird tears strips from palm leaves and weaves them into a hollow ball. The oven bird lives in open country in Argentina and Paraguay, where trees are few. So it uses fence posts and bare branches as sites and builds a nest of mud which looks like an oven. The male hornbill walls up the female in a hole in a tree by building a mud wall across the entrance leaving only a tiny hole in the centre. Through this he passes food to his mate as she incubates the eggs and later to the nestlings as well. Cave swiftlets in southeast Asia nest in caves but since there may not be enough ledges, they build artificial ones with their spit, sometimes mixed with a few feathers or roots.

Several species, of which the cuckoo is the most famous, avoid the dangers and drudgery of incubation altogether by laying their eggs in the nest of some other bird and allowing it to rear the young. To avoid having their eggs thrown out by the foster parents, they lay eggs that look very like those already in the nest.

At last, the young hatch. They chip their way out of their shells with a small egg-tooth on the tip of their bills. Many of those that nest on the ground are covered with down when they hatch and this gives them excellent camouflage. Almost as soon as they are dry, they run to search for food while their mother guards them. Chicks in nests above ground are usually naked and helpless at first and have to be fed by their parents.

As the days pass, their feathers sprout. Young eagles and storks, as they grow feathers, may spend days standing on the edge of their nests, beating the air with their wings. They strengthen their muscles and practise the movements necessary for flying. Gannets on their narrow cliff ledges do the same thing, facing inwards just in case they become too successful too early. Such preparations, however, are the exceptions. Most young birds seem to be able to fly with no practice. Some that are raised in holes, like petrels, manage to fly several kilometres at their first try and almost all young birds become accomplished flyers within a day or so.

Astonishingly, despite their skill in the air, birds appear to abandon flight whenever possible. The older fossil birds, living some 30 million years after Archaeopteryx, included gull-like birds which were skilled flyers. They were like modern birds. With them, however, lived a huge swimming bird, Hesperornis, which was nearly as big as a human adult. It had already given up flying. Fossils show that those other highly successful non-flying birds, the penguins, also appeared around this time.

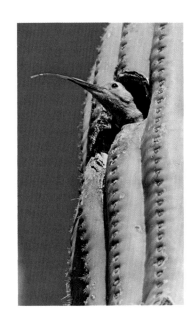

Nests in holes
The flicker (*above*) is a member of the woodpecker family. It cuts nesting holes not only in cactuses, as this one has done, but in tree trunks and even telegraph poles. The oven bird (*below*) constructs its own nest hole by building a hollow globe of mud which dries as hard as brick in the sun. Inside the entrance, a wall half-crosses the interior and acts as a barrier against raiders.

Lords of the air

This return to ground-living can still be seen today. When a species of land bird colonizes an island where there are no four-footed hunters, sooner or later it seems to become flightless. Rails on the islands of the Great Barrier Reef can only flutter feebly into the air if in danger. The cormorants of the Galapagos have such small wings that they cannot get in the air even if they try. On the islands of the Indian Ocean, huge flightless pigeons developed – the dodo on Mauritius and the solitaire on Rodrigues. Unfortunately for them, their islands did not remain without hunters for ever. A few centuries ago, humans arrived and within a short time exterminated them both. In New Zealand too, there were no hunters before the arrival of humans and several bird groups developed flightless forms. The moas, the tallest birds that have ever existed, standing over 3 m high, were hunted to extinction by early humans. Only their small relatives, the kiwis, survive from the whole group.

Flying uses a lot of energy. If a bird can stay on the ground in safety then this is a much easier way of life and birds will adopt it. It must have been to escape from land-living reptiles that Archaeopteryx took to the trees in the first place and the threat of hunting mammals that has kept its descendants there ever since.

But in between these two periods, there was a gap of a few million years when the dinosaurs and most reptiles had disappeared and the mammals did not yet rule the land. It seems that birds did then make a bid to claim the ruling position for themselves. 65 million years ago, an immense flightless bird called Diatryma stalked the plains of Wyoming. It was a hunter. Taller than a man, it had a massive hatchet-shaped bill easily able to butcher large creatures.

Diatryma disappeared after a few million years, but giant flightless birds still survive elsewhere – ostriches, rheas and cassowaries. They are not close relatives of Diatryma but they are descended from birds that once flew. The cassowaries give us some idea of how impressive Diatryma must have been. Their feathers are like coarse hair and their stubby wings are armed with a few curving quills as thick as knitting needles. On their heads they have a bony crest with which they force their way through the thick vegetation of the New Guinea jungles where they live. They feed on fruit but they also take small creatures such as reptiles, mammals or nestling birds. Apart from poisonous snakes, they are by far the most dangerous creatures on the island. When cornered, they lash out with savage kicks that can rip open a person's stomach and many people have been killed by them. They are convincing evidence that if large flesh-eating birds should develop a taste for bigger prey, they could be very dangerous.

Yet in the end, birds like Diatryma were not clever enough hunters. One group of animals escaped them. They were small creatures at that time but they were very active. Like the birds, they had developed warm blood but they insulated themselves not with feathers but with fur. They were the first mammals. It was their descendants which inherited the earth and kept the birds, by and large, in the air.

A dangerous bird
The cassowary of New Guinea.

9 · Eggs, pouches and placentas

At the end of the eighteenth century, the skin of an astounding animal arrived in London from Australia. The creature to which it had belonged was about the size of a rabbit, with fur as thick as an otter's. Its feet were webbed and clawed. It had a single rear opening for reproduction and disposing waste, like that of a reptile. And most outlandish of all, it had a large flat beak like a duck.

When complete specimens became available, it was seen that the bill was not hard and bird-like as it had at first seemed, but soft and leathery. So it was not really like that of a bird. The fur was much more significant. Hair or fur is the hallmark of a mammal, just as feathers are of a bird. It was clear, therefore, that this mystery animal must be a member of that great group which contains creatures as different as shrews, lions, elephants and humans. The purpose of a mammal's hairy coat, like the feathers of a bird, is to insulate the body and enable it to maintain a high temperature, so it followed that this new creature must also be warm-blooded.

The Australian colonists called the creature a 'water-mole' but scientists named it Platypus, which means 'flat-footed'. Soon afterwards, it was realized that this name had already been given to a flat-footed beetle, so the animal was relabelled Ornithorhyncus, 'bird-bill'. This is now its scientific name but most people still call it a platypus.

It lives in the rivers of eastern Australia, swimming energetically, paddling with its webbed forefeet and steering with its hind. When it

A platypus

dives, it closes its ears and tiny eyes with little flaps of skin. Unable to see as it grubs around on the river bed, it feels for freshwater prawns, worms and other small creatures with its sensitive bill. As well as being a good swimmer it is also a powerful burrower, digging tunnels through the river banks sometimes as much as 18 m long. Here the female makes an underground nest of grass and reeds. From one of these there eventually came more sensational news about the animal. It was claimed that the platypus laid eggs.

Many zoologists in Europe regarded this as being ridiculous. No mammal laid eggs. If eggs were found in a platypus nest, then they must have been laid there by some other visiting creature. They were described as being nearly round and soft-shelled, in which case they were probably those of a reptile. But local people in Australia insisted that they belonged to the platypus. Then in 1884, a female was shot just after she had produced an egg. A second was found inside her body. Now there could be no doubt. Here was a mammal that did indeed lay eggs.

Further surprises were to come. After 10 days, these eggs hatch, but the young are not left to find food for themselves as all young reptiles must do. The female develops on her belly some special glands. They are similar to the sweat glands that the platypus, like most animals, has elsewhere on its skin to help cool the body if it gets overheated. But the liquid these glands produce is thick and rich in fat. It is milk. It oozes into the fur and the young suck it from tufts of hair. There is no nipple, so the platypus cannot be said to have a true breast or mamma, the feature which gives the mammals their name – but it is a beginning.

The other important trait of a mammal – warm-bloodedness – also seems to be only partly developed. Nearly all mammals keep their bodies at temperatures between 36°C and 39°C. The platypus's temperature is only 30°C and varies a great deal.

There is one other creature in the world with this mixture of primitive mammalian and reptilian features – the echidna or spiny anteater. It also lives in Australia. The animal looks like a large flattened hedgehog with spines on its back embedded in a coat of dark bristly hair. It can dig itself into the ground with swimming movements of its four legs when it needs to escape attack. But the animal is not mainly a burrower. It spends most of its time either asleep or waddling through the bush searching for ants and termites. When it finds a nest of them, it tears it open with the claws of its front legs. Then it licks up the insects with a long tongue which flickers in and out of the tiny mouth at the end of its tube-like snout.

The echidna's snout and its spines, like the bill of the platypus, are details that have developed to suit its particular way of life. Basically, the echidna is very similar to the platypus. It has hair, its body temperature is very low, it has a single rear opening and it lays eggs.

In one detail of its reproduction, it differs. The female keeps her eggs not in a nest, but in a pouch which develops for a time on her

A short-nosed echidna
This species lives in most parts of Australia.

A long-nosed echidna
This species comes from the huge island of New Guinea, to the north of Australia. It has a much longer snout and legs than its Australian relative and only a few spines in its thick coat of bristly hair.

belly. When the moment for laying arrives, she curls round and manages to deposit her eggs directly into the pouch. The shells of the eggs are moist and stick to the hair in the pouch. After seven to ten days, they hatch. Thick yellowish milk oozes from the skin of the mother's belly and the young suck it up. They remain in the pouch for some seven weeks by which time they are about 10 cm long and their spines have begun to develop. The mother now scoops them out and deposits them in a den. She continues to suckle them for several more weeks.

The only food a reptile mother provides for its baby is the yolk in its egg. From this small yellow ball, the young reptile must build a body that is sufficiently complete and strong to make it totally independent as soon as it hatches from the shell. It must then go and seek food for itself. The platypus uses a method that has greater possibilities. Its eggs have a small amount of yolk in them but by feeding its young with milk as soon as they hatch, it enables them to have a much longer development. This feeding of the young is a major change in maternal care and one that has been very important for the success of the whole mammal group.

The echidna and platypus are undoubtedly very ancient animals, but we have no hard evidence to show which fossil reptiles were their ancestors. Nonetheless, it is a reasonable guess that the kind of breeding techniques they use today was developed by some reptile groups whose descendants eventually became mammals.

A young echidna
Its spines are just beginning to grow and it has left its mother's pouch.

The forerunners of the mammals

In the rocks of Texas, dating from some 270
million years ago, there are fossils of reptiles
which had huge sails on their backs. They
lived in an arid desert country and were
vegetarians, feeding on the early cone-
bearing trees like the ones shown growing
near the cliffs in the background.

The sails on their backs probably served as
a way of regulating their body temperature. If
the animal stood broadside onto the sun in the
early morning, it could gather heat and warm
its blood very quickly so that it could become
active early in the day. It seems that such
creatures as these may well have been the
ancestors of the first mammals.

Also in the picture are some amphibians.
The pair on the right belong to a species
which probably stayed close to water.
Sheltering under a boulder on the left is
another kind. This was very reptile-like and
may well have had a thick skin so that it could
live for most of its life in the dry desert and
only had to return to water to breed.

But which reptiles were they? The hallmark of today's mammals – hair, warm blood and milk-producing glands – do not fossilize. But other things can suggest that an animal had warm blood. As we have already seen, some dinosaurs, such as Stegosaurus, developed very effective methods of absorbing heat from the sun. But they were not the first reptiles to do so. An earlier group, sailbacks, also managed to do this with a sail of skin supported on long spines from their backbones. The sailbacks later lost their sails. It is difficult to believe that they lost such a valuable thing as warm blood. It is more likely that their sails disappeared because they had managed to produce heat within their bodies, and so no longer needed sails with which to absorb it from the sun. Warm-bloodedness needs some form of body insulation if it is to be effective, so it could be that some of these descendants of the sailbacks were covered in fur.

Whatever their exact ancestry, true mammals began to appear some 200 million years ago. A small fossil, discovered in 1966 in southern Africa, is the earliest example so far found. It was only about 10 cm long and somewhat shrew-like. Details of its jaw and skull link it firmly with true mammals. Its teeth were suited to eating insects and it must have been both warm-blooded and furry. We cannot tell whether it laid eggs like a platypus or gave birth to live young and suckled them by means of a breast. The mammals, however, had now certainly arrived.

Even so, the next great developments among the land animals did not come from them. Instead, the dinosaurs began their dramatic expansion. But the mammals survived, saved by their warm blood, which allowed them to be active at night when the great reptiles became sluggish. It must have been then that they came out from hiding and hunted for insects and other small creatures. This situation continued for 135 million years but when the dinosaurs disappeared, 65 million years ago, the little mammals were ready to take over.

Among them were creatures that were very like the opossums that today live in the Americas. The Virginia opossum is a large rat-shaped creature with a long naked tail which it can wrap round a branch with enough strength to support its own weight. It has a large mouth that it opens alarmingly wide to show a great number of small sharp teeth. It is a tough adaptable creature that has spread through the Americas, from Argentina in the south to Canada in the north. It feeds on fruit, insects, worms, frogs, lizards, young birds – almost anything that is edible.

The most extraordinary thing about it is the way it reproduces. The female has a large pouch on her belly in which she rears her young. It is called marsupium, meaning 'little bag', and all the creatures which have one, including the opossum, are known as marsupials.

Opossums, like the echidna and platypus, have a single rear opening which is used for reproduction and disposing waste. When they mate, the male fertilizes the female's eggs inside her body. The developing young or embryos that result have only tiny yolk sacs to

A Virginia opossum

143

Young opossums
(*Below*) 15 days old, clinging to the teats within their mother's pouch. (*Above*) after ten weeks, the young climb out of the pouch and cling to their mother's back.

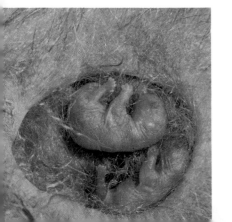

provide them with food and it does not last long. After 12 days and 18 hours they enter the world – blind, pink and no bigger than bees. They are so unformed that they cannot really be called babies, and are called instead by the special name of neonate. The female may produce as many as two dozen of them at a time. As they come out of their mother's opening, they haul themselves through the fur of her belly to the pouch, a distance of about 8 cm. It is the first and most dangerous journey of their lives and half of them may well die on the way. Once they reach the warmth and safety of the pouch, each fastens onto one of the 13 nipples and starts to suck milk. If more than 13 complete the journey, the latecomers will starve and die because there are no more nipples. Nine or ten weeks later, the young clamber out of the pouch. They are now fully formed, the size of mice, and cling to their mother's fur. It is three months before they leave her and set off on an independent life of their own.

Playing possum
When it is attacked, an opossum
often becomes paralysed and
seems to be dead, with its eyes
closed and its mouth hanging open.
Then suddenly it will recover and
run away.

**An opossum mother with her three-
month-old babies**

Eggs, pouches & placentas

A marsupial cat – the quoll from eastern Australia

The earliest fossil marsupials found so far come from South America and it may be that the group originated here. But the greatest number of marsupials today live not in America but in Australia. How could they have got from one continent to the other?

To find an answer to that question, we have to return to the period when the dinosaurs ruled. At that time, the continents of the world were connected to one another. Fossils of dinosaurs have been found in all of today's continents and the early mammal-like reptiles were also widespread. But towards the end of the dinosaur's reign, this great land split into two – a northern supercontinent made up of Europe, Asia and North America and in the south, another made up of South America, Africa, Antarctica and Australia.

The great southern landmass eventually began to break up. Africa separated and drifted northwards. Australia and Antarctica remained joined to one another and were linked to the southern tip of South America. At this time the marsupials were probably developing in South America, and they spread across into the Australian-Antarctic landmass.

Meanwhile, primitive mammals were also appearing in the northern supercontinent. They were to develop a different way of nourishing their young. Instead of moving them at a very early stage into an outside pouch, they kept them within the body of the female and nourished them by means of an organ called the placenta. We can look at this technique later. For the moment it is enough to know that this different branch of the mammals existed.

The South American marsupials flourished while they had the continent to themselves. A huge wolf-like form appeared and also a leopard-like carnivore with sabre-like teeth. But South America drifted slowly northwards and connected with North America by way of a land bridge near Panama. The placental mammals from the north came down this corridor of land into South America. They challenged the marsupials for food and space and most of the marsupials died out. Only the tough opossums were left. Some of these colonized North America, as the Virginia opossum has done today.

The marsupials that lived in the central part of the southern

A Tasmanian devil
This is the largest of the marsupial cats about 50 cm long. Extinct on the Australian mainland, it is found today only on the island of Tasmania.

supercontinent, however, fared even worse. They did not survive at all, for this great block of land became Antarctica. It drifted over the South Pole where it was so cold that life became impossible for the marsupials. The creatures on the third section of the supercontinent, however, were luckier. This was Australia. It drifted into the Pacific and remained totally separate from any other continent. So the marsupials there have developed for the last 50 million years cut off from the rest of the world.

During this vast period, they produced a great number of different types. You can see the remains of some of the spectacular species that once existed in the limestone caves of Naracoorte, 250 km south of Adelaide. The floor is covered with a soft red silt, carried down here by an underground river that has long since disappeared. With the mud, it brought the bones. Some were of marsupials that had lived in the upper cave. Others appear to have been from creatures of the surrounding forests that had accidentally fallen into the cave. The bones lie thick on the mud – leg bones, shoulder blades, teeth and skulls. There are the remains of a huge marsupial the size and shape of a rhinoceros and of an immense kangaroo with a head like a small giraffe that browsed on the branches of trees. These creatures died about 40,000 years ago. We do not know why but it may be that they were affected by changes in the climate, for Australia continued to drift northwards and so slowly became warmer and drier.

Great numbers of marsupials still survive, of course. Today there are nearly 200 species. Many of these creatures look at first sight like placental animals from the northern hemisphere. The colonists who came to Australia from Europe understandably gave the marsupials the names of the European creatures they most closely resembled. When the colonists found little furry, pointed-nosed, long-tailed creatures, they called them marsupial mice. The name is misleading for these are not timid rodents but savage hunters that will attack insects quite as large as themselves. There are meat-eating marsupials that will hunt reptiles and birds and are called marsupial cats. There was also a marsupial wolf, the thylacine. This creature was a very efficient hunter. It took to feeding on the newly introduced sheep

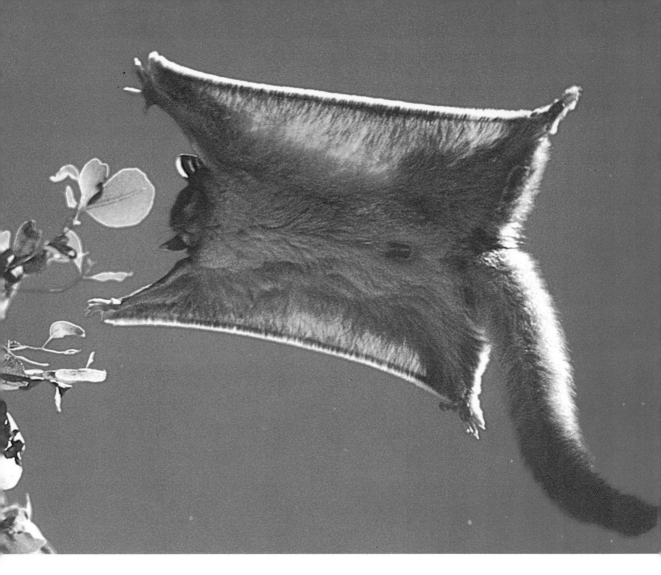

Similar gliders
(*Above*) the sugar glider, a marsupial from eastern Australia; (*below*) the flying squirrel, a placental mammal from North America.

(*Opposite*) **a koala with young**

and was itself hunted and eventually exterminated by farmers. The last identified living one died in the London Zoo in 1933, but there is still a chance that a few might survive in the remoter parts of Tasmania.

In two cases the placental and marsupial forms are so similar that you can hardly see the difference. The sugar glider is a small marsupial that lives in eucalyptus trees. It has a parachute of skin connecting its fore- and hind legs which enables it to glide from branch to branch. It looks very like a North American flying squirrel which is a placental. Both the marsupials and the placentals have produced a creature that burrows underground. We call both moles. Both kinds have short silky fur, tiny eyes, powerful digging forelegs and a stumpy tail. The female marsupial mole, however, has a pouch for her young.

But a similar life style does not always produce marsupials and placentals that look like one another. The koala is a medium-sized creature that lives in trees feeding on leaves, as monkeys do elsewhere. But the slow-moving, plodding koala neither looks nor

Eggs, pouches & placentas

A numbat
(*Upper right*) numbat neonates in the pouch; (*lower right*) an adult numbat.

(*Above*) **a honey possum**

(*Below*) **a rat-kangaroo: the boodie**

behaves like the active intelligent monkey. The numbat is an anteater. It has the long sticky tongue that all anteaters use to collect their food, but it does not have the long curving tube for a snout as the great anteater of South America does. One marsupial, the honey possum, has no placental equivalent at all. It is only the size of a mouse, its jaws are pointed and it has a tongue with a brush on the end of it with which it licks nectar and pollen from flowers.

In the cool woodlands of Tasmania lives another creature which is also unique, the boodie. It is one of a small group of marsupials called rat-kangaroos. It is very shy and comes out only at night, feeding on all kinds of food, including meat. It makes its nest in a burrow. To collect material it picks up straws in its mouth, stacks them in a pile on the ground and then pushes them back under its long tail with its hind legs. The tail then curls up tightly so that the straw is bundled and the boodie moves away with it. To do so, it hops. Boodies move about entirely on their back legs, which have very long feet. If you had to design a creature to serve as a primitive ancestor of the most famous Australian animal of all, the kangaroo, it might well look like the boodie.

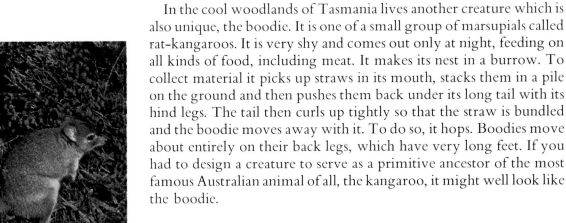

A kangaroo

The development of the kangaroo family was hastened by the drying and warming of Australia. This caused the forest that had covered most of the land to thin and be replaced by more open grassland. Grass is good food, but to move out of the forest and graze in the open is to be exposed to attack by hunting animals. So any grass-eater had to be able to move fast. The kangaroos managed that with a greatly improved version of the boodie method. They hopped – and magnificently.

No one knows why kangaroos do this rather than running on all fours as grazing creatures do elsewhere in the world. Maybe, if you are carrying babies in a pouch, it is easier to hop with an upright body than to run on all fours. Whatever the reason, the kangaroos have brought the hop to a peak of efficiency. They can reach speeds of 60 km/h and clear fences of 3 m high.

The second difficulty that grass-eaters must overcome is the wear and tear on their teeth. Grazers elsewhere have teeth that grow as they wear down. Kangaroo teeth do not do this. Instead there are four pairs of cheek teeth on either side of the jaws. Only the front ones are used. As they are worn down to the roots, they fall out and

Eggs, pouches & placentas

those from the rear move forward to take their place. By the time the animal is 15 or 20 years old its last teeth are in use. When these have worn down and fallen out, the animal will die of starvation.

There are some 40 different species in the kangaroo family. The smaller ones are usually called wallabies. The largest is the red kangaroo, which stands taller than a human adult and is the biggest of all living marsupials.

Kangaroos reproduce in much the same way as the opossums. The egg is produced and waits in the uterus, the organ in the female's abdomen where the embryo develops. The female mates, the egg is fertilized and begins its development. If this is the first time that the female has mated, it does not stay there long. In the case of the red kangaroo it is only 33 days before the neonate comes out. Usually only one is born at a time. It is a blind, naked worm a few centimetres long. Its hind legs are mere buds. Its forelegs are better developed and with these it hauls its way through the thick fur of its mother's belly. The neonate's journey to the pouch takes about three minutes. Once there it fastens onto one of the four nipples and starts to feed. Almost immediately, the mother's sexual cycle starts again. Another egg is produced, she mates again and the egg is fertilized. But then an extraordinary thing happens. The egg's development stops. Meanwhile, the neonate in the pouch is growing quickly. After 190 days, the baby is large enough to make its first trip out of the pouch. From then on it spends more and more time in the outside world and eventually, after 235 days, it leaves the pouch for good.

Young wallabies
(*Below*) a neonate two days after it arrived in the pouch; (*right*) 65 days old.

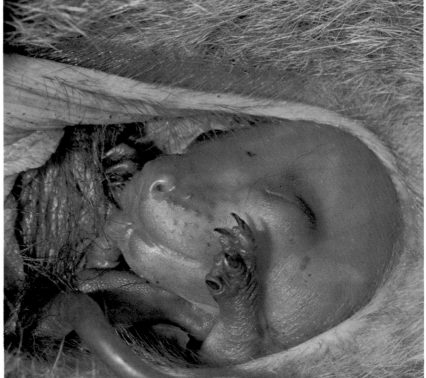

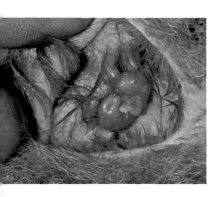

If there is a drought at this time, as happens so often in central Australia, the fertilized egg in the uterus still remains undeveloped. But if there has been rain and there is good pasture, then the egg restarts its development. 33 days later, another bean-sized neonate will wriggle out of the mother's opening and make its way up to the pouch. The female will then immediately mate again. But the first born does not give up its milk supply so easily. It returns regularly to feed from its own nipple. So now the female has three young dependent on her. One active young which grazes but comes back to suckle; a second, the tiny neonate, sucking at her teat in the pouch; and a third, the fertilized but undeveloped egg, within her uterus.

It is commonly thought that the marsupials are backward creatures, scarcely much of an improvement on those primitive egg-layers, the platypus and echidna. That is a long way from the truth. The marsupial method of reproduction must certainly have appeared very early in the history of mammals, but the kangaroos have developed it marvellously. No other mammal anywhere can compare with the female kangaroo who, for much of her adult life, supports a family of three in varying stages of development.

A mammal's body is a very complicated machine that takes a long time to develop. Even as an embryo it is warm-blooded and burns up fuel very quickly. This means that the developing young has to be supplied with considerable quantities of food. Mammals have found a way of providing far more nourishment by means of the placenta than could ever be packed within the yolk of an egg.

A red kangaroo with young
The baby, called by this stage a joey, is about 7 months old and climbs in and out of her pouch.

A red kangaroo with young
The joey is now about 8 months old
and can no longer get into the
pouch. But it stays close to its
mother and sticks its head inside
her pouch to suckle.

The placenta is a flat disc attached to the wall of the uterus. It is connected by the umbilical cord to the developing baby or foetus. Blood itself does not pass from mother to young. But oxygen from her lungs and nourishment from her food, both dissolved in her blood, are carried through the umbilical cord to the foetus. There is also traffic in the other direction. The waste products produced by the foetus are absorbed by the mother's blood and then disposed of through her kidneys.

The placenta allows the young to remain within the uterus until they are well developed. In some cases they are fully mobile as soon as they are born. Even after this, they are provided with milk until they can gather food for themselves. The placental breeding technique spares the young the dangerous journey outside their mother's body at a very early stage that a marsupial has to undertake. It also allows their mother to supply their every need during the long period they remain within her. So whales and seals can carry their unborn young even as they swim for months through freezing seas. No marsupial with air-breathing neonates in a pouch could ever do such a thing. It was this placental technique that was to prove one of the main causes of the mammal's success in colonizing the whole of the earth.

10· Insect-eaters and others

Sit quiet and still in a forest in Borneo and you might see a small, furry, long-tailed creature running through the branches and over the ground, testing everything with its pointed nose. It looks and behaves like a squirrel. But if, when it finds something to eat, it does not nibble at it with its front teeth but opens its mouth wide and champs with huge relish, then you are watching something much more unusual than a squirrel – a tupaia.

The tupaia might well resemble the ancient creature from which all placental mammals are descended. Judging from fossil skeletons, the first mammals that scampered about in the forests with the dinosaurs must have looked very like it – small, long-tailed and with a pointed nose, a furry coat, warm-blooded, active and insect-eating.

The reign of the reptiles had been a long one. They had come to power about 250 million years ago. They had browsed the forests and munched the lush vegetation of the swamps. Meat-eating dinosaurs had developed and preyed on the plant-eaters. Other species lived by eating leftovers from the hunters. Plesiosaurs and ichthyosaurs cruised the seas seeking fish and pterosaurs glided through the skies. And then, 65 million years ago, all these creatures disappeared. The forests of the world lay still. No great beasts of any kind crashed their way through them. But in the undergrowth those small tupaia-like mammals, that had been there when the dinosaurs first appeared, were still hunting for insects.

A tupaia

Insect-eaters and others

Primitive insect-eaters
(*Upper right*) a shrew from Europe; (*right*) a spiny tenrec from Madagascar; (*below*) a female European shrew with her young.

The tupaia is only one of these primitive insect-eating mammals that have survived until today. There are others scattered around the world in odd corners. In Malaysia lives an irritable creature with a long nose bristling with whiskers and smelling of rotten garlic that is known as a moon rat. In Africa there is the biggest of all which is called an otter shrew because it swims and some creatures the size of rats which hop, have slender legs and trunk-like noses and which are known as elephant shrews. And Madagascar has a whole group called tenrecs, some striped and hairy, some with spines on their backs.

Not all of them are rare. That common animal of the European countryside, the hedgehog, is another of them. Apart from its coat of spines it is not unlike the rest. And there are also the shrews. In many

parts of the world they are very plentiful, scurrying through the leaf litter in hedgerows and woodlands in a fever of excitement. Although they are only about 8 cm from nose to tail they are very ferocious, attacking any small creature they meet including one another. To keep up their energy, they have to eat great quantities of earthworms and insects every day. Among them is one of the smallest of all mammals, the pigmy shrew that is so tiny that it can squeeze down tunnels no wider than a pencil. Shrews communicate with one another by shrill high-pitched squeaks. They also produce noises too high for human ears to hear. Their eyesight is very poor and it seems that they use these high-pitched sounds as a simple form of echo-location.

Insect-eaters and others

A European hedgehog
(*Upper right*) a female with young.
She may have as many as seven
babies. (*Lower right*) a hedgehog
curled up in defence.

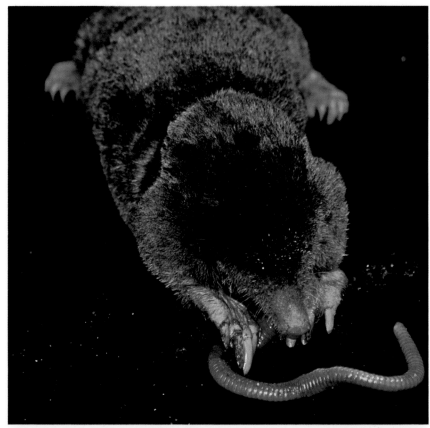

Moles
(*Upper left*) a European mole with its favourite food, an earthworm; (*lower left*) a star-nosed mole from North America. The flower-like feelers around its nose help it find its way through the darkness of its tunnel.

The shrew group has produced one creature that seeks its prey entirely underground, the mole. Eyes are of very little use underground. Even if there were any light to see by, they would easily clog with mud, so the mole's eyes are very small. Nonetheless, a mole must have some way of finding its way about. At the front, its main sense organ is its nose, covered with many sensitive bristles and used for both smell and touch. At the rear, it has a short stumpy tail also covered with bristles which tells it what is happening behind.

Insect-eaters and others

The tunnels moles make are not simply passageways but traps. Earthworms, beetles, insect larvae, burrowing through the soil, may suddenly break into a tunnel. The mole, scurrying along its passages, harvests whatever turns up. It patrols its entire network at least once every three or four hours and eats vast numbers of worms each day. Sometimes so many worms collect in the tunnels that even a mole's appetite is satisfied. Then it gathers up the rest, gives each of them a quick bite to paralyse them, and stores them away in an underground larder. Some of these stores have been found with thousands of worms in them.

A few insect-eaters have specialized in eating ants and termites. A long sticky tongue is the best tool for this job. The numbat, the marsupial anteater in Australia, has one. So has the echidna. Even ant-eating birds, woodpeckers and wrynecks, have developed one that fits inside a special compartment of the skull. But the longest tongues of all are those developed by the ant-eating placental mammals.

A European mole
(*Right*) the mole's tunnel serves as a trap into which worms fall.
(*Below*) the mole pushes the earth it digs out of its tunnel up to the surface as a mound. Sometimes it clambers out above ground itself.

A tree pangolin from Africa
This female has a baby clinging to her.

In Africa and Asia, there are seven different kinds of pangolin, creatures about 1 m long with short legs and long grasping tails. The biggest of them has a tongue that can stick out 40 cm beyond its mouth. The pangolin has lost all its teeth and its lower jaw is only thin blades of bone. The ants and termites are collected by the mucus on the tongue, swallowed and then mashed by the stomach.

Because it cannot move quickly and it has no teeth, the pangolin has to be well-protected. It has an armour of horny scales that overlap like tiles on a roof. At the slightest danger, the animal tucks its head into its stomach and wraps itself into a ball with its tail clasped tight around it. There is no way in which a pangolin, once rolled, can be forced to unwind. If you want to see what it looks like, the only thing to do is to leave it and let it recover enough confidence to poke its head out and then trundle away.

Insect-eaters and others

A nine-banded armadillo
This is the most widespread kind of armadillo. It lives over most of South America and has; within the last hundred years, moved north into central America and beyond to Texas.

A hairy armadillo
This species digs holes both as dens in which to live and in search for food such as termites.

South America has its own groups of insect-eaters. The armadillos, like the pangolins, are protected by armour. This consists of a broad shield over the shoulders and another over the hips with a varying number of half-rings over the middle of the back. Armadillos eat insects, other invertebrates, and sometimes other small creatures like lizards. They usually seek food by digging. They have an excellent sense of smell and when they detect something edible in the ground, they start digging with frantic speed, scattering earth behind them. Their noses are jammed into the soil as though they are terrified of losing the scent and desperate to get a mouthful of food as soon as they possibly can. When you watch them, you wonder how they can possibly breathe. In fact they do not. They have the amazing ability to hold their breath for up to six minutes, even while digging.

Today, there are some 20 species of armadillos. Once there were a lot more, including a monster with a shell as big as a small car. One such fossil shell has been found which, it seems, was used by early humans as a tent. The biggest surviving species is the giant armadillo, the size of a pig, which lives in the forests of Brazil. In Paraguay, the little three-banded armadillo trots about on the tips of its claws and can roll into a neatly fitting ball. In Argentina there are tiny hairy ones that are mole-like and seldom come above ground. All armadillos have teeth. The giant has about 100 but they are small and peg-like.

The specialist anteaters of South America, like the pangolins of Africa, have lost their teeth entirely. There are three of them. The

Three South American anteaters
The pygmy anteater (*above*) lives in trees and rears up like this to defend itself. The giant anteater (*left*) roams over the plains. This female has a young one clinging to her. The tamandua (*below*) is medium-sized and finds its food both in the trees and on the ground.

smallest, the pygmy anteater, lives in trees and only eats termites. It is about the size of a squirrel with soft golden fur and curving jaws which form a short tube. A bigger version, the tamandua, is cat-sized, has a grasping tail and short coarse fur. It too is a tree-dweller but it often comes down to the ground. Out on the open plains lives the biggest of the trio, the giant anteater. It is 2 m or so long. Its tail is huge, shaggy and flag-like and waves in the breeze as the animal shambles over the grasslands. Its forelegs are bowed, and its claws so long that it has to tuck them inwards and walk on the sides of its feet. With these claws it can tear open termite hills as though they were made of paper. Its toothless jaws form a tube even longer than its forelegs. When it feeds, its huge tongue flicks in and out of its tiny mouth and goes deep into the termite hill.

All anteaters are fairly slow movers. Since they lack teeth as well, they appear defenceless and it seems strange that they should be without the kind of armour that both the pangolins and armadillos have. But the pygmy anteater and the tamandua spend most of their time up in the trees out of the way of most hunters. And the giant anteater is less harmless than you might think. If you go to lasso one, it will lash at you with its forelegs. If it caught you with its huge hooked claws, there would be little chance of your breaking loose. There is a tale of the bodies of a jaguar and an anteater being found out on the grasslands, locked together. The anteater had been dreadfully torn by the jaguar's teeth, but its claws were sunk in the jaguar's back and even in death its clutch on its attacker had not been broken.

Insect-eaters and others

A colugo
(*Right*) This female has her young
cradled on her belly. She carries it
like this even when she flies.
(*Below*) a colugo gliding.

All these creatures collect crawling insects. But insects also fly. The first insects took to the air some 300 million years ago and they had it to themselves until the arrival of the flying reptiles like the pterosaurs, some 100 million years later. Whether the reptiles flew at night we do not know, but it seems unlikely because when their bodies cooled at night they would not be able to produce enough energy to do so. Birds eventually followed them, but there is no reason to suppose that there were any more night-flying birds in the past than there are today – which is very few. So a great feast of insects awaited any creature that could manage to fly in the dark. One group of the insect-eating mammals did so.

We have some idea of how the mammals may have taken to the air. In Malaysia and the Philippines there lives an animal called the colugo. It is about the size of a large rabbit but its entire body is covered by a furry cloak of skin. The colugo uses this membrane to glide through the air.

The colugo is not the only gliding mammal. Some squirrels plane through the air in just the same way. But the colugo has the biggest membrane. It took to gliding early in the history of mammals and shows a state that some early insect-eaters probably passed through on their way to becoming those expert flyers, the bats.

That development took place very early, for fossils of fully-developed bats have been found that date back 50 million years ago. The bat's flying membrane stretches not just from the wrist, like the colugo, but along the long second finger. The other two fingers also help support the skin. Only the thumb remains free. This has a nail

An insect-eating bat (*above*)

A colony of bats in a cave (*left*)

and the bat uses it for grooming and to help it clamber about.

Like birds, bats have very light bodies. The bones in the tail are thinned to mere straws to support the flying membrane or have been lost altogether. Though they have not lost their teeth, their heads are short and often flat-faced and so avoid being nose-heavy in the air. Bats have one problem that the birds are not troubled with. Their mammal ancestors did not lay eggs but bore live young. The female bat must fly with the heavy load of her developing baby within her. It is not surprising to find that bats rarely have twins and usually only one young is born each season. This means, in turn, that the females must breed for many years if the population is to remain the same. Indeed, bats are surprisingly long-lived creatures for their size. Some live up to 20 years.

To fly at night, bats had to develop a special way of navigating in the dark. It is based on sounds like those made by shrews that are so high-pitched we cannot hear them. The bats use them for sonar, a method of echo-location. This is similar to radar, except that radar used radio waves whereas sonar uses sound waves. A bat sends out these click-like sounds in short bursts, 29 or 30 times every second. Its hearing is so sharp that from the echo each signal makes, the bat can tell the position of obstacles around it and of its prey.

If the bat's mouth is filled by an insect, it cannot squeak properly. Some species avoid this difficulty by squeaking through their noses and have grotesque growths around their nostrils which act like miniature megaphones. The echoes are picked up by the ears. These are also very sensitive and may be twisted to search for signals.

The strange faces of bats
(*Below*) an African horseshoe bat; (*bottom*) a wrinkle-faced bat from Panama.

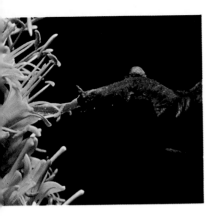

Not all bats feed on insects. Some have discovered that nectar and pollen are very nutritious. They can hover like hummingbirds in front of flowers and gather nectar by probing deep into the blossoms with long thin tongues. Just as a great number of plants use insects as pollinators, so others rely on bats. Some cactus, for example, only open their blossoms at night. Their scent is strong and the flowers stick up above the spines so that the bats are able to visit them without damaging their wings.

The biggest of all bats live on fruit. They are called flying foxes, not only because of their size – some of them have a wingspan of 1.5 m – but because their coats are reddish brown and their faces are very fox-like. They have large eyes but only small ears, so it is clear that they do not use sonar. Fruit bats roost in the tops of trees in colonies tens of thousands strong, and may travel as far as 70 km in their search for food.

A nectar-feeding bat (*above*)
The ancestors of this bat probably visited flowers just to collect the insects gathered there. Then they too began to sip nectar from the flowers and now they have long tongues to help them do so more easily.

A fruit bat – the flying fox
(*Right*) In flight, the finger bones that support the wing can be clearly seen. (*Below right*) an Australian flying fox feasting on bananas.

Other bats have taken to feeding on meat. Some prey on roosting birds, some take frogs and small lizards, one is reported to feed on other bats. One American species even manages to fish. At dusk, it flies over ponds, lakes or even the sea. The bat tucks up its tail and trails its feet in the water. Its toes are large and armed with hook-shaped claws. When they strike a fish, the bat scoops it up into its mouth and kills it with a powerful crunch of its teeth.

The vampire bat has become very specialized. Its front teeth are like two triangular razors. It settles gently on a sleeping mammal, a cow or even a human being, and shaves the skin so that blood oozes out. Then the vampire squats beside the wound lapping it up.

All in all there are nearly 1000 species of bats. They have made homes for themselves in all but the very coldest parts of the world. They must be counted as one of the most successful of the descendants of the insect-eaters.

A vampire bat
(*Left*) in flight; (*below left*) having bitten a donkey, the vampire crouches beside the wound and laps the dripping blood; (*below*) the special teeth with which the vampire cuts the skin of its victims.

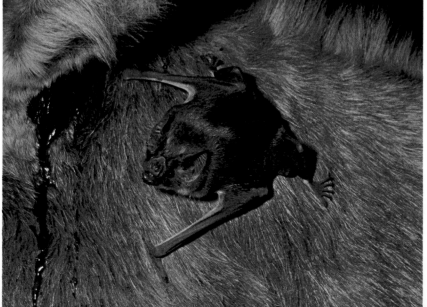

Insect-eaters and others

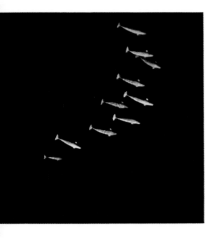

A school of white whales seen from the air

A humpback whale leaping

Whales and dolphins are also warm-blooded, milk-producing mammals. They too have a long ancestry, with fossils dating back to 50 million years ago. It is hard to believe that these immense animals are also descended from a tiny creature like a tupaia but their ancestors must have entered the sea at a time when the only other mammals in existence were the insect-eaters. Their bodies are now so well adapted to swimming that they give no clues as to how that move into the sea was made.

The forelimbs have become paddles. The rear limbs have been lost altogether, though there are a few small bones buried deep in the whale's body to prove that it once had back legs. They have lost their fur and instead have developed blubber, a thick layer of fat beneath the skin that prevents their body heat from escaping even in the coldest seas.

The mammals' need to breathe air is a real handicap in water, but the whale has developed a way of breathing more efficiently than most land-living animals. It only has to take a breath at very long intervals. The finback whale, for example, can dive to a depth of 500 m and swim for 40 minutes without drawing breath.

One group of whales has specialized in feeding on tiny shrimp-like crustaceans called krill, which swarm in the sea. Just as teeth are of no use to mammals feeding on ants, so they are no use to those eating krill. So these whales, like anteaters, have lost their teeth. Instead they

have baleen, sheets of horn, feathered at the edges, that hang down from the roof of the mouth. The whale takes a huge mouthful of water containing krill, half shuts its jaws and then presses out the water with its tongue. The krill remains in the mouth and is then swallowed. On such a diet, the baleen whales have grown to an immense size. The blue whale, the biggest of all, grows to over 30 m long and weighs as much as 25 bull elephants. There is an advantage to a whale in being large. Maintaining body temperature is easier the bigger you are. The dinosaurs gained the same advantage by growing big but their size was limited by the strength of bone. Above a certain weight, their limbs would break. The whales, however, do not have this problem for their bodies are supported by water. Nor do they need to move quickly to filter krill. So the baleen whales have developed into the largest living creatures that have ever lived on earth, four times heavier than the largest known dinosaur.

The toothed whales feed on different prey. The largest of them, the squid-eating sperm whale, only reaches half the size of the blue whale. The smaller ones, dolphins, porpoises and killer whales, hunt both fish and squid and have become extremely fast swimmers, able to reach speeds of over 40 km/h. Moving at such speeds, navigation becomes very important. Fish are helped by the pores on their sides that are sensitive to pressure, but mammals lost that far back in their ancestry. Instead, the toothed whales use sonar like bats.

The teeth of a killer whale

A baleen whale
When the humpback feeds, it takes a huge mouthful of water (*below left*). Then it presses out the water with its tongue through the sheets of baleen (*below*) which line its upper jaw. So it filters out the small creatures which are its food.

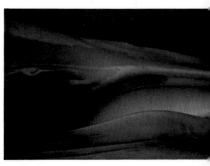

Insect-eaters and others

Apart from these high-pitched sounds, dolphins produce a great variety of other noises that some people believe are part of a language. So far, we have identified some 20 different sounds. Some seem to serve to keep a school together when they are travelling at speed. Some appear to be warning cries, and some call-signs so that animals can recognize each other at a distance. But no one yet has proved that dolphins put these sounds together to form the two-word sentence that can be regarded as the beginning of true language. Chimpanzees can do so. But dolphins, as far as we can tell, cannot.

The great whales also have voices. Humpbacks, which are baleen whales, gather every spring in Hawaii to give birth to their young and to mate. Some of them also sing. Their songs consist of yelps, growls, high-pitched squeals and long drawn-out rumbles. A complete song lasts for about ten minutes, but some have been recorded that continue for half an hour. Whales may sing, continuously repeating their songs, for over 24 hours. Each whale has its own song but it composes it from themes which it shares with the rest of the whale community.

We still do not know why whales sing. Humans can identify each individual whale by its song and if we can do so, then surely whales can do the same. Water carries sound better than air so it may well be that these songs can be heard by other whales up to 50 km away. Perhaps the songs inform other whales of the whereabouts and activities of the rest of the whale community.

So the descendants of the early insect-eaters developed into creatures as big as whales and as small as bats as they specialized in eating different kinds of small invertebrates.

Dolphins
(*Above*) they are friendly, inquisitive and easily tamed; (*below*) travelling at speed, they often leap out of the water.

11· The hunters and the hunted

The forests of today are very much the same as those that developed soon after the appearance of the flowering plants, 50 million years ago. The dinosaurs had fed on them, but when they all disappeared, a calm settled over the forests of the world. The peace continued for thousands of years but eventually, the small warm-blooded furry animals that had been running at the feet of the dinosaurs, snapping up small invertebrates, began to develop a taste for new foods. While some hunted insects, others fed on leaves.

Eating plants is no easy business. For one thing, vegetable matter is not very nutritious. An animal has to eat great quantities in order to get the energy it needs. Some vegetarians have to spend three-quarters of their waking hours gathering and chewing leaves and twigs. Out in the open, they are exposed to attack. One way for an animal to reduce that risk is to grab as much food as possible and run off with it to somewhere safe. That is what the giant West African rat does. At night when there seems to be least danger, it comes out from its burrow and stuffs its cheek pouches with anything edible. Seeds, nuts, fruits, roots, sometimes a snail or a beetle, all go in. The pouches are so large that they can hold about 200 such morsels. When both sides are crammed full and the rat can barely shut its mouth, it scurries back to its burrow. Below ground it empties the collection in its larder and begins to feed.

Plant-eaters need to have good teeth. Not only do they have to use them for very long periods but the plants they chew are often very tough. Rats like other rodents – squirrels, mice, beavers, porcupines – have front gnawing teeth that continue to grow throughout the animal's life as they wear down.

Teeth for gnawing
A young grey squirrel tackles a nut.

A leaf-feeder
A rabbit usually feeds at dusk and dawn or at night. It can eat $\frac{1}{2}$ kg of leaves every 24 hours.

Once gnawed and swallowed, the food has to be digested. This, too, presents problems. The material from which the cell walls of plants are built is very tough. Digestive juices alone cannot break it down. So plant-eaters have bacteria in their stomachs which help to break down the food for them. Even with the help of bacteria a vegetarian meal can take a long time to digest.

The rabbit has an unusual solution. Its meal of leaves, having been chewed and swallowed, goes down to the stomach where it is attacked by bacteria and digestive juices. Then, it passes down into the gut, is moulded into soft pellets and excreted. This usually happens when the rabbit is resting in its burrow. As soon as the pellets come out, the rabbit turns round and swallows them. Once more they go down to the stomach and the last bits of nourishment are taken out. Only after this second processing are the pellets deposited outside the burrow as waste.

Elephants have special problems for they eat a great deal of twigs and woody material. Apart from their tusks, their only teeth are grinders at the back of the mouth. These teeth crush with enormous power, but even so, the elephant's food is so woody it takes a very long time to digest. A meal eaten by a human being normally passes through the body in about 24 hours. An elephant's takes about two and a half days to make the same journey and for most of that time it is kept stewing in the digestive juices of the stomach. That means that the elephant must have a huge stomach and this may be one reason why these animals have grown so big. Plant-eating dinosaurs also grew huge, probably for this reason among others.

The most complicated way of digesting plants is the one used by

antelope, deer, buffalo as well as sheep and cows. They clip grass from their pasture with their front teeth. They then swallow it quickly and it goes down to the rumen, a part of the stomach which contains bacteria. There it is churned about for several hours, and broken down into a mash. Eventually, the mash is brought back up into their mouths a bit at a time to be chewed thoroughly by the back teeth. This cud-chewing can be done when the animal has left the feeding grounds and is resting in a safe place. Eventually, the mouthful is swallowed for the second time. It goes past the rumen and onto the main part of the stomach. Now at last the animal gains some benefit from all its work.

Leaves have one further shortcoming as food. In cooler parts of the world, they disappear in the winter. The creatures that depend upon them must therefore make special preparations as winter approaches. Asiatic sheep turn their food into fat and store it around the base of their tails. Other species not only feed and fatten themselves as much as they can, but they also hibernate or sleep through the winter.

A dormouse in autumn is almost round. It finds a hole, screws up its eyes, tucks its head into its stomach, wraps its tail around itself and goes to sleep. Its heartbeat slows and its breathing becomes so shallow that you can hardly notice it. The muscles stiffen and the body feels as cold as stone. In this state the animal needs very little energy to stay alive and gets it from fat stored in its body. When spring comes, the warm weather brings the dormouse and other winter sleepers out of their holes. Their appetites are huge, for they may have lost as much as half of their body weight during the winter. But starvation is over. The leaves once more are sprouting.

A browser
The African elephant eats a lot of grass, tearing it up in whole clumps with its trunk. But it also browses on trees, eating whole branches, complete with twigs and leaves, and stripping bark from the trunk.

A dormouse in its winter sleep

The hunters and the hunted

With such methods as these, a great variety of animals nourish themselves on the vegetable foods provided by the forests of the world. Up in the topmost branches, squirrels scamper along the twigs, collecting bark and shoots, acorns and catkins.

One of the first creatures to move up into the branches in South America was the sloth. There are two main kinds of sloth, the two-toed and the three-toed. Of these, the three-toed is the more slothful or lazy. It hangs upside-down from a branch by hook-like claws at the ends of its long bony arms. It feeds on only one kind of leaf which is plentiful and easily found. No hunters attack the sloth – few indeed can reach it – and nothing competes with it for food. It sleeps 18 hours every day. It pays such little attention to its grooming that green algae grow on its hair and moths live in its mouldy coat. It cannot move at a speed of over 1 km/h even over the shortest distances and the swiftest action it can make is a sweep of its hooked

A three-toed sloth
This female has a baby cradled on her stomach.

arm. Its hearing is so poor that you can let off a gun within inches of it and it will just turn slowly and blink. So plant-eating has led the sloth into a life very close to a continuous sleep.

The forest floor is not rich in vegetation. In some areas the shade is so dense that there is nothing but a layer of rotting leaves. Elsewhere, if the trees are thinner, there may be small bushes, a few herbs and some saplings. In Africa and Asia, such plants provide food for small antelope – the mouse deer and the duiker. About the size of dogs, they are extremely shy. Primitive cud-chewers very like them were among the first leaf-eaters to wander through those forests of 50 million years ago.

In South America, low vegetation on the forest floor is eaten not by hoofed animals but by rodents, the paca and agouti. They are the same sort of shape and size and if anything they are even more nervous and shy.

Grazers on the jungle floor
The agouti from South America (*above*) and the mouse deer from Asia (*below*) look very alike, but the agouti is related to rats and the mouse deer to antelopes.

The hunters and the hunted

Jungle browsers

The okapi (*below*) is an antelope that lives in the thick forests of central Africa. The tapir (*right*) is related to the rhinoceros. This kind lives in South America. Another is found in Asia.

A hunter of the woodlands

The weasel (*below*) feeds mostly on voles and mice but it also takes eggs, nestling birds and young rabbits.

Browsing on the taller shrubs and saplings needs greater height and every forest has a small population of creatures, ranging in size from ponies to horses, that do so. They are so secretive, silent, and few in number that they are hardly ever seen – in Malaya and South America, the tapirs, which are active at night; in parts of southeast Asia, the Sumatran rhinoceros, the smallest of all its kind and now very rare; and in the Congo, the okapi, a short-necked cousin of the giraffe.

All these ground-living forest dwellers are solitary creatures. The reason is clear. The shaded forest floor rarely produces enough leaves to feed a large group in one area. So the mouse deer, the agouti and the tapir live in pairs or by themselves. They have territories which they mark with dung or scent from a gland and they rely on hiding for their defence.

The hunters that seek them are also solitary. The jaguar stalks the tapir, the leopard pounces on the duiker. A wandering bear will eat most things and will tackle a mouse deer if it gets a chance. The smallest of the hunters – genets, jungle cats, civets, and weasels – pursue rats and mice as well as birds and reptiles.

Of all the hunters, the cats are the most specialized for meat-eating. Their claws are kept sharp by being drawn back into sheaths. When they attack, they hook their victim with them and then deliver a piercing bite in the neck that cuts the spinal cord and brings a swift death. The long dagger-like tooth on either side of the mouth, typical of a meat-eater, is used to slash open the skin of the prey. The jagged ones farther back in the jaw cut bones. None of the dogs or cats can really chew. Most bolt their food in hunks. This does not cause problems because flesh is easier to digest than leaves or twigs.

These nightly duels of ambush and flight have been going on between the plant-eater and the beast of prey ever since the first forests. But some 25 million years ago there was an important change. Grasslands appeared and plant-eaters left the forests and came out into the open.

With no place to hide, they made tempting targets for beasts of prey. Only the largest of the vegetarians, the elephants and rhinoceros, had nothing to fear. Their great bulk, together with their tough skin, protected them from even the most powerful flesh-eater. But for smaller creatures the plains were filled with danger.

Grazers on the plains
These black rhinoceros live in the open plains of Africa, but other kinds of rhinoceros, living in Asia, are forest dwellers.

Some sought safety in burrows. Grasslands are marvellous places for creatures with a taste for tunnelling. The ground is free from tangling tree roots, so here they can tunnel with ease. The plains of North America are colonized by rodents the size of small rabbits called prairie dogs. They not only graze above ground but do so during the day when coyotes, bobcats, ferrets and hawks are about – all creatures that will kill a prairie dog if given the chance. Prairie dogs have developed defences which depend upon a highly organized social system.

They live in huge groups called towns which may contain as many as 1000 animals. Each town is divided up into a number of communities of about 30 individuals, all of whom know one another well. Many have linking burrows. There are always some members on guard duty, sitting upright on the mound of excavated earth beside the burrow entrance where they can get the best view. If one spots an enemy, it lets out a series of whistling barks. The call is repeated by others nearby and so spreads through the town, putting everyone on guard. The inhabitants do not flee but take up positions close to their holes. From there, standing on their hind legs, they stare at the intruder, watching its every move. So as a coyote trots through the town, it is met with fixed glares from the citizens who let it come close before they duck into their burrows.

The social life of the prairie dog is not limited to defence. During the

Prairie dogs in their town
(*Above*) on sentry duty beside the entrance to the burrow; (*below*) ready for a quick retreat to safety below ground.

breeding season, the group members keep to themselves and defend their boundaries against any intruders. When this time is over, they become more relaxed. Citizens move about the town, wandering into one another's areas. If a stranger approaches a resident, the animals cautiously exchange a kiss and then inspect one another's glands beneath the tail to see if they are acquainted. If they are not, then they separate and the visitor departs. But if they discover that they are members of the same group, then they kiss open-mouthed, groom one another and often move off to graze side by side.

Further south, on the grasslands of Argentina, the role of the prairie dog is taken by a guinea pig the size of a spaniel called the viscacha. They, too, live in communities but they graze only at dusk and at dawn. Like many creatures that are active in the twilight, they have bold marks, black and white stripes across the face. They build mounds over their burrows. If they find a stone during their diggings they drag it up to the surface and dump it in a pile on the top.

In North America, a different group of grass-eaters developed on the prairies. Their ancestors were forest-living creatures, not unlike tapirs but smaller. On the plains they began to run faster and faster in order to escape their enemies. The first forms had four toes on the front legs and three on the hind. The longer the limbs, the faster they can carry their owners. As time passed these grazers lengthened their legs by rising off the ground onto their toes. Eventually, the side toes

Prairie dogs in their town
(*Above*) grooming one another; (*below*) an adult proclaims its ownership of a burrow by whistling and at the same time making a little leap into the air.

The hunters and the hunted

Zebras
These are plains zebras, the commonest of these African wild horses. Another kind, with thinner stripes, live in dry mountainous country. Behind them, waiting their turn to drink at the water hole, stand oryx, one of the bigger antelopes.

disappeared and the animals were running on a single middle toe protected by a thick nail or hoof.

These animals also grew large heads to provide room for the large teeth they needed to chew the tough grass. So they developed into the horses we know today. They spread across the plains of America and eventually into Europe, at a time when the Bering Strait was dry so that the two continents were joined. From there the early horses spread south to the plains of Africa. Later, they died out in their original American home and only reappeared there 300 years ago when they were shipped across by the Spanish conquistadors. But in Europe and Africa, they flourished as horses, donkeys and zebras.

The zebras share the African plains with other running grazers which had been developing separately. They were the descendants of the miniature forest antelopes. They had also lengthened their legs for running by rising on their toes, though they did so on two not just one like the horse. They became the cloven-hoofed grazers – antelope, gazelle and deer.

On the edges of the plains in the open bush, where there is still a little cover to be had, the antelope of today – dik-dik and duikers – remain very like their forest-dwelling relations. They are small,

browse on shrubs and live alone or in pairs on territories that they mark and defend. Farther out in the open, where there is nowhere to hide, the antelope seek safety in numbers, gathering together in large herds. They lift their heads regularly from grazing to look around. With so many sharp eyes and sensitive nostrils on guard, it is hard for a hunter to take the herd by surprise.

The herds have to keep on the move to find fresh pasture. But this wandering life complicates breeding arrangements. In the forest, a single pair had lived by themselves on their territory. For some of the plains-living antelopes – the impala, springbok and gazelles – territory still remains the basis of their arrangements. Males and females form separate herds. A few bucks will leave the bachelor herd to set up individual territories for themselves. Each marks the boundary of his land, defends it against other males and tries to attract females into it and mate with them. Other plains-living grass-eaters – the eland, the largest of the antelopes, and the plains zebra – have given up all claims to a particular patch of land for breeding. They form herds in which both sexes are always present and the males settle their problems over females by battling between themselves wherever the herd happens to be.

A herd of impala
As they run, they make bounding leaps, which may help to confuse an attacker, preventing it from concentrating on one individual.

Plains zebra stallions fighting

In order to catch the grazers, the hunters on the plain have had to improve their own running techniques. They have not developed hooves, perhaps because have always needed their toes, armed with claws, as weapons. Their solution is different. They have lengthened their limbs in effect, by making their spines very flexible. Travelling at high speed, the spine bends so far that the hind and front legs overlap one another beneath the body just like those of a galloping antelope. The cheetah has a thin long body and is the fastest runner on earth, capable of reaching speeds of over 110 km/h. But its method of running takes a great deal of energy and the cheetah cannot keep up such speeds for more than a minute or so. Either it outruns its prey within a few hundred metres and makes a kill, or it has to retire exhausted, while the antelope continue to gallop off to a safer part of the plains.

A cheetah at speed
This animal has just finished one bound. As it takes another, its supple body will bend so far that its hind legs will hit the ground between its front legs.

A cheetah pursuing a Thomson gazelle

The end of a hunt
One of these cheetahs has killed a zebra foal. Now the whole family is feasting on it. The rest of the zebra herd seems to know that the danger has passed for the moment and stands watching.

The hunters and the hunted

Leopard
Leopards usually hunt alone and at night. This one (*below*), unusually, is chasing a pig during the day. After it has killed and taken a first meal, it often hauls the remains of its victim into a tree (*above*) where jackals and hyenas cannot get it.

Lions are nowhere near as fast as the cheetah. Their top speed is about 80 km/h. A wildebeest can do about the same and keep it up for much longer. So lions have had to develop more complicated ways of hunting. Sometimes they rely on stealth, creeping towards their victims, their bodies close to the ground. Sometimes, an individual hunts by itself. But on occasion, members of a pride or family will work as a team – and they are the only cats that do so. They set off in line abreast. As they approach a group of their prey – antelope, zebra or wildebeest – those lions at the ends of the line move a little quicker so that they begin to encircle the herd. Finally, these break cover, driving the prey towards the lions in the centre of the line. This often results in several of the team making kills.

Hyenas are even slower than lions. The best they can manage is about 65 km/h so their hunting depends even more on teamwork. They usually hunt at night. Sometimes they set off in small groups of two or three looking for wildebeest. They test the herds by charging them and watching the fleeing animals closely, trying to spot any weakness among individuals. In the end they appear to choose one animal and begin to chase after it, snapping at its heels until it finally turns to face its pursuers. When it does that, it is doomed. While it faces one hyena, another lunges at its belly, sinks in its teeth and holds on. The wildebeest is now crippled. So its guts are ripped out and within a minute or so it is dead.

Lions
Lions live in family groups called prides. The lionesses do most of the hunting, sometimes by themselves, sometimes working as a team. Here they have killed a zebra and their cubs have trotted up to join in the meal.

The hunters and the hunted

Hyenas
A hyena is not big enough or fast enough to bring down an animal as big as a zebra by itself. But when hyenas work as a team, a zebra is very lucky to escape.

Zebra are more difficult prey. To hunt them, the hyenas unite to form a large team. When they are in groups like this, they will trot straight past herds of wildebeest, paying no attention to them. At last they sight a zebra and the hunt begins. Zebras run in family groups of half a dozen or so, led by the head stallion. He sounds the alarm with a braying danger call. As the herd gallops away, he takes up the rear, placing himself between the pursuing hyenas and his mares and foals. The hyenas follow in a crescent behind. The stallion will swerve and attack the pack with powerful kicks and bites and even chase the leading hyena. But eventually one of the pack will get past the stallion and begin to snap at a mare or a foal. As the chase continues, one gets a tooth-hold on a leg or the belly and the animal is dragged down. While the rest of the terrified zebra run to safety, the hyenas leap on the fallen animal, howling and whooping, ripping it to pieces. Within a quarter of an hour, the entire body – hide, guts and bones, everything except the skull – will have disappeared.

So the speed of the zebras and antelopes demanded teamwork from the hunters. That response came not only from members of the cat and dog family. Other kinds of animals also came out on the grasslands to hunt. One group of them was particularly slow and poorly armed so that for them teamwork and communication were even more important. Eventually they became the most clever and communicative of all the hunters on the plains. To trace their history, we have to return to the forest, for it was there that they had their origins, searching for fruit and leaves in the tops of the trees.

12· A life in the trees

If you want to clamber about in trees, it is useful to be able to do two things: to judge distances, and to hold onto branches. Two forward-facing eyes that can both focus on the same object can provide the first, and hands with grasping fingers, the second. About 200 living species have that pair of talents. They include monkeys, apes and ourselves and we call the whole group the primates.

There is no doubt that the early tupaia-like mammals, which were the ancestors of such different creatures as bats, whales and anteaters, also gave rise to the primates. The tupaia does not yet have either of the primate hallmarks. Its hands have long fingers, but it cannot touch any of its fingers with its thumb, so it has not got a true grasp. Furthermore, each finger ends with a sharp claw, not a flat nail. Its eyes are large but they are placed on the sides of its long snout so that their fields of vision only partly overlap. The animal has not yet become a true climber. One or two tupaia species run along branches like squirrels, but most of them spend much of their time on the ground. With one exception, they are all active during the day. When you watch them scuttling about through the undergrowth, it is easy to see that they rely very much on their sense of smell.

Smell is also the basis of their social life. They use it to find their food. They mark their territories with little drops of urine and with scent from glands. Their noses are very long and sensitive, ending with two comma-shaped nostrils that are surrounded by bare moist skin like the muzzle of a dog. All in all, the tupaia seems a very unlikely creature to be related to a monkey. But there is a whole group of primates which share some of its characteristics and which are unmistakably monkey-like in other ways. These show how the transformation might have taken place. They are called the prosimians or 'pre-monkeys'.

A typical prosimian is the ring-tailed lemur of Madagascar. It is sometimes called the cat lemur, for it is cat-sized and one of its calls sounds like the miaow of a cat. But there the resemblance ends. It is not a hunter but is largely vegetarian like many prosimians.

Ring-tails often travel on the ground in troops. Scent plays a very important part in their lives. Their noses are not so well-developed as those of a tupaia, but they are still very fox-like. They also have moist muzzles with bare skin around the nostrils. They have three kinds of scent glands – one pair on the inside of the wrist which opens through horny spurs, another close to the armpits, and a third around the sexual organs. With these, the males and to a lesser extent the females, produce lots of signals. As the troop moves through the forest, the animals mark trees by rubbing their scent glands on the bark. The male ring-tail uses scent not only as a marker but as an attacking weapon. When he prepares for battle with a rival, he rubs his wrists

A ring-tailed lemur

A life in the trees

Tail-waving
When they are on the ground, ring-tailed lemurs hold their vividly-marked tails high like banners. They also use them to waft smells at one another in stink-fights.

against his armpit glands. Then he brings his tail forward between his hind legs and in front of his chest and draws it several times between his wrist spurs so that it is covered with scent. Thus armed, rivals face each other on all fours. They lift their haunches high and thrash their splendid tails over their backs so that the smell is fanned forwards at each other.

The ring-tail also spends a lot of its time in trees. Here its primate characteristics show their value. The eyes on the front of its head give it a binocular view. Its grasping hands with their mobile fingers and thumbs grasp branches, and its fingers ending in short nails enable it to pluck fruit and leaves from the tips of branches.

The ability to grip is put to good use by the baby lemur which is able to cling to its mother's fur as soon as it is born. It travels with her wherever she goes. Mothers often sit about in groups together, grooming and resting on the forest floor. The young will then scramble happily from one female to another.

The ring-tails' limbs are all about the same length, so that when they run on the ground they do so on all fours. There are, however, over 20 different kinds of lemurs in Madagascar and most of them spend nearly all their time in trees. The sifaka, a beautiful creature a little larger than the ring-tail with pure white fur, has become a specialist in jumping. Its legs are considerably longer than its arms and enable it to leap 4 or 5 m from one tree to another. However, it is unable to run on all fours. On the few occasions when it does come down to the ground, it has to stand upright and hop with both feet together.

The most tree-living of the group is the indri, a close relation of the sifaka. It is the biggest of all living lemurs with a head and body nearly 1 m long. Its legs are even longer in proportion than those of a sifaka. Its big toes are widely separated from the rest and about twice the length, so that the animal can grasp even thick trunks between its toes. It is the most magnificent jumper of all, launching itself upright, in soaring bounds which it can repeat again and again so that it seems to bounce its way from trunk to trunk through the forest.

Indris also use scent in marking the trees, though less than the ring-tail. Instead, they have another way of claiming their ownership of territory. They sing. Every morning and evening, a family fills its patch of forest with an unearthly wailing chorus. When they are alarmed, they lift their heads and trumpet a different hooting call which carries for great distances through the forest. This use of sound does have one disadvantage. It gives away the animal's position to any enemy that might be seeking it. But up in the branches, no natural enemy can reach the indri and so it can sing without fear.

Although the ring-tail, sifaka, indri and several other Madagascan lemurs are active during the day, their eyes can see in very dim light. This is strong evidence that these lemurs were once mostly active at night. Many others of their relatives in Madagascar still are.

The gentle lemur, which is about the size of a rabbit, lives in holes in trees. When darkness comes, it moves about with exaggerated slowness. The smallest of the group is the mouse lemur, with a snub nose and large appealing eyes, that scampers through the thinnest twigs.

Larger lemurs
Some lemurs are little bigger than mice, but others, like the sifaka (*above left*) and the indri (*above right*) are the size of monkeys. One species, now extinct, was as big as a gorilla.

A life in the trees

The rarest living lemur; the aye-aye
There may be only about 50 of these very extraordinary lemurs left alive.

Prosimian prowlers of the night
1 Bushbabies. There are six different kinds of bushbabies or galagos in Africa. This is the medium-sized one which is the most common. It lives in dryish woodlands and bush country.
2 The potto lives in the rain forests of west Africa. It is a slow-moving creature, about the size of a cat, which feeds mostly on leaves and fruit. **3 The angwantibo** also lives in the west African forests but eats mostly insects. **4 The mouse lemur** of Madagascar is one of the smallest of all prosimians. It eats insects, fruit and leaves. **5 The slow loris** is a forest dweller which is found in many parts of southeast Asia. It always moves very slowly and feeds on a very wide variety of food, both animal and vegetable.
6 The slender loris comes from Sri Lanka and south India. It lives mostly on insects, small lizards and birds.

Oddest and most specialized of all is the aye-aye. Its body is about the size of an otter. It has black shaggy fur, a bushy tail and large paper-thin ears. One finger on each hand is long and bony. With this the aye-aye picks out beetle larvae, its main food, from holes in rotten wood.

50 million years ago, there were lemurs and other prosimians not only in Madagascar, but in Europe and North America. Around 30 million years ago, after Madagascar was separated from the continent of Africa, more advanced primates developed. They also lived in trees and fed on fruit and leaves and were in direct competition with the lemurs. They never reached Madagascar, however, so the lemurs continued to live there unchallenged. Elsewhere, the lemurs lost the competition with the monkeys. But not totally, for all living monkeys, with the single exception of the South American douracouli, are only active during the day. Some of the prosimians that are active at night still survive.

In Africa, there are several kinds of bushbaby, very similar to mouse lemurs, as well as the potto and the angwantibo. These last two are like the gentle lemurs and move very slowly. In Asia, there is a spindly creature, the slender loris from Sri Lanka, and the rather larger and plumper slow loris. Although all these creatures have quite large eyes, they still mark their trees with scent and use it for route-finding in the dark.

The tarsier
Its extremely long legs enable it to make great leaps. Although it is only about the size of a rat, it can easily jump 2 m in a single bound.

One more prosimian lives in the forests of southeast Asia, the tarsier. It is the size and shape of a small bushbaby. It has a long near-naked tail tufted at the end, very long leaping legs and long-fingered grasping hands. But the briefest glimpse of its face is enough to show that it is a very different creature from the bushbaby. It has gigantic glaring eyes. They are 150 times bigger in proportion to the rest of its body than our own. As well as these spectacular eyes, the tarsier has paper-thin ears, like those of a bat, that can be twisted to focus on a particular sound. With these two highly developed sense organs it hunts at night for insects, small reptiles and even birds.

It marks its territory with scent, but after watching it hunt, it is clear that vision is just as important to it as the sense of smell. A look at its face shows that the animal is quite different from all other prosimians. For one thing, the eyes are so huge that there is little room for the nose itself. The nostrils are not comma-shaped nor are they surrounded by bare moist skin, as are the noses of other prosi-

mians. In this it resembles monkeys and apes. In fact, the tarsier seems
to be a close relative of those early primates which, 50 million years
ago, spread through the world displacing most of the prosimians and
populating both the Old World and the New with monkeys.

Monkeys differ from all the prosimians, except the tarsier, in that
sight is more important to them than smell. It is obviously very
valuable for creatures living in trees to be able to see where they are
going. So daylight suits them better than darkness and all monkeys,
except for the douracouli, are active at that time. Their eyesight is
better than that of prosimians. Not only do they see in depth, they
have greatly improved colour vision. With such good eyes they can
judge the ripeness of distant fruit and the freshness of leaves. And
they can use colour in their communications between one another.

In Africa there lives de Brazza's monkey which has a white beard,
blue spectacles, orange forehead and black cap, and the mandrill with
a scarlet and blue face; in China, the snow monkey with a golden

A life in the trees

coat and blue face; in the Amazon forests, the uakari with a scarlet naked face. These are among the most spectacularly costumed monkeys but a great number of other species also have coloured fur and skin. With these adornments they advertise their sex and species and threaten rivals. So monkeys have themselves become the most highly coloured of all mammals because their colour vision is so good.

They also use sound a great deal, for up in the trees they are beyond the reach of most hunters. Howler monkeys in South America sit morning and evening and sing in chorus. This sound can be heard for several kilometres and is said to be the loudest noise produced by any animal. But all monkeys have a varied repertoire of noises. There is no such thing as a dumb monkey.

The monkeys that reached South America and became isolated there developed along their own lines. All of them have flat noses with widely-spaced nostrils opening to the side. Monkeys in the rest of the world have thin noses with forward or downward pointing nostrils.

One South American group, the marmosets and tamarins, still use

The uakari
Three different kinds of uakari live in the South American forests. All are bald with naked faces. As well as this one, with reddish brown fur, there is another scarlet-faced species with whitish fur. The third has brown fur and a black face.

scent a great deal in communication even though they are active during the day. The males gnaw the bark of a branch and then soak it with urine. But they also have elaborate adornments – moustaches, ear-tufts and crests – with which they show off and they threaten one another with high-pitched calls. The way they rear their young also seems primitive, for it is like the lemurs. The babies move from adult to adult and often gather on a long-suffering father.

Marmosets are the smallest of all true monkeys. They have taken up a way of life that is more like that of a squirrel, eating nuts, catching insects and licking sap from bark. The pygmy marmoset has a body length of only 10 cm. Since they are so small, they run along branches rather than clamber between them. Their hands are not big enough to grasp the branches. So the nails that their ancestors had developed have changed back again to claws with which they can cling to bark.

The marmosets, however, are exceptional. Most monkeys are very much larger. But greater weight makes increased demands on those grasping hands and the South American monkeys have developed another way of holding on. They have turned their tail into a fifth grasping limb. It has special muscles so that it can curl and

Marmosets and tamarins
There are over 30 different kinds of marmosets and tamarins, all belonging to one family. Most have vivid fur patterns and colours. The emperor tamarin (*above*) grows a huge moustache. The lion marmoset (*left*) has a mane and coat of golden fur that has a magnificent metallic glint.

A life in the trees

A fifth limb
Spider monkeys (*above and right*) have a patch on the end of their tails which is without fur and covered with tiny ridges that leave prints just like fingerprints. They can grip just as firmly with their tails as they can with their hands.

Swimming for food
The crab-eating macaque (*below*) lives in mangrove swamps and beside creeks in southeast Asia. It catches not only crabs but shrimps and molluscs.

grip. It is so powerful that a spider monkey can hang by its tail while gathering handfuls of fruit with both hands.

African monkeys, for some reason, have never developed their tails in such a way. They do use their tails to help them balance when running and jumping. Even so, the African monkey's tail is hardly as useful to it as the grasping tail of its South American cousin. Maybe the failure of the African monkeys to develop their tails as climbing aids has meant that they found life in the trees increasingly difficult as they grew larger and so began to spend more time on the ground. It is certainly true that there are no ground-living monkeys in the New World, whereas in the Old World there are many.

The ground-living macaque is one of the most successful of all primates. If you wanted to pick a monkey that was bright, adaptable and tough, the macaque would be the best choice. There are about 60 different kinds and between them they stretch halfway around the world. One group, the only wild non-human primates in Europe, lives on Gibraltar. Another macaque species, the rhesus, is one of the commonest monkeys in India, often living around temples where it is held to be sacred. Farther east still, a macaque has become a good swimmer, paddling and diving in the mangrove swamps in search of crabs and other crustaceans. In Malaysia, the pig-tailed macaque is often trained to climb palm trees and pick coconuts for its human

Swimming for warmth
In one part of Japan, the macaques warm themselves during the winter by bathing in hot volcanic springs.

masters. The most northerly of all monkeys is another macaque, living in Japan where it has developed a long and shaggy coat to protect it from cold winters.

Receiving images from two very good eyes and putting them together to form one detailed picture required an enlargement of the brain. So did the ability to link what the animal saw with the movements of the hands and fingers. And a monkey brain, compared with a lemur brain, is bigger in other ways. The part that enables an animal to learn has also grown.

The Japanese macaques show how good monkeys have become at learning. Several troops of them have been studied by Japanese scientists. One lives in the mountains of northern Japan where the snow lies thick in winter. Observers watched a troop of monkeys move into a part of the forest that none of them had explored before. It contained some hot volcanic springs. The monkeys found that the warm water could provide a delicious bath. A few tried it. Soon the habit spread. Now they take hot baths every winter.

In 1952 when scientists began to study another group of macaques on the small island of Koshima, the animals were wild and shy. In order to draw them out into the open, the scientists began to feed them with sweet potatoes. In 1953 a young female, whom the observers had named Imo, picked up a sweet potato as she had done many times before. As usual, it was covered with earth and sand, but Imo, for some reason, took it down to a pool, dipped it in the water and rubbed off the dirt with her hand. A month later, one of her companions began to do the same. Four months later, her mother did so. The habit spread among the members of the group. Some began to use not just freshwater pools but seawater. Today washing sweet potatoes in the sea is a universal habit. The only individuals that never learned it were those that were already old when Imo made her first experiment. They were too set in their ways to change.

But Imo was not finished with her discoveries. The scientists also regularly threw down handfuls of rice on the beach, thinking that it would take the monkeys so long to pick out the grains there would be plenty of time to observe them. They had not reckoned on Imo. She grabbed handfuls of the rice, sand and all, scampered away to a rock pool and threw them into the water. The sand dropped to the bottom but the rice floated and she skimmed it off with her hand. Once again the habit spread and soon everyone was doing it. This readiness to learn from your companions results in a community having shared skills, knowledge and shared ways of doing things – in short, what we call culture.

Feeding the Koshima macaques has led to another development. The researchers simply tip a sack of sweet potatoes on the beach and withdraw. Many macaques rush to the pile, grab a root with one hand, stuff another in the mouth, and hobble off on three feet. A few, however, do better. They gather up several roots, clutch them to their chests with both arms and then manage to run across the beach standing upright on their hind legs. If this daily feeding continued over many generations, it is easy to see that the major share of food

Standing upright
Many monkeys, like this macaque, are able to stand upright on their hind legs when they want to get a clear view or carry something in their hands.

A learned skill
A Japanese macaque mother on Koshima Island has learned from others in the troop how to wash her sweet potato. Her baby watches her doing it and will almost certainly do the same when it grows up.

would go to those monkeys that could balance on their hind legs. These would be better fed and dominate the group. They would reproduce more successfully and their characteristics would become widespread in the group. So, over a few thousand years macaques might become increasingly two-footed. Such a change did happen to some primates in Africa some 30 million years ago.

At that time, one group of lower primates were increasing in size. This brought a change in the way they moved through the trees. Instead of balancing on the top of a branch and running along it, they began to swing along beneath it. Swinging demands physical changes. The arms lengthened, for the longer they are the better they can reach. The tail no longer played any part in balancing and so it disappeared. The muscles and skeleton changed in order to support an upright body. Those changes produced the first apes. Today four main kinds of ape survive: the orang-utan and the gibbon in Asia, the gorilla and chimpanzee in Africa.

The great red-haired orang of Borneo and Sumatra is the world's heaviest tree-dweller. A male may stand over 1.5 m tall, have arms with a spread of 2.5 m and weigh a massive 200 kg. The fingers on all four limbs have powerful grips, so that the animal is best described as being four-handed. The hip joints are so loose that an orang can stick its legs out at angles that are impossible for humans.

At the same time, their size does seem to be something of a handicap. Branches break under their weight. Often they are unable to get fruit they want because it is hanging on a branch that cannot support them. Moving from tree to tree can also cause problems. Sometimes an old male gets so large that he finds moving through the trees too exhausting. When he wants to travel any distance he

An orang utan mother with her baby

A jungle acrobat
When the gibbon swings through the trees, it holds its fingers to form a hook so that it can quickly and easily latch onto a branch and off again. Its thumb is very low on the hand, close to the wrist, so that it is well out of the way.

comes down and lumbers across the forest floor. Males live a solitary life, travelling and eating by themselves and only seeking company when they mate. Female orangs are about half the size of their mates but they too are unsociable animals and travel through the forest accompanied only by their young. This preference for solitude may well be connected with their size. Orangs are fruit-eaters, and being so big, have to find large quantities of it every day. Fruiting trees are scarce and widely scattered through the forest. So the orangs have to make long journeys, continually searching, and they may find it better to keep their discoveries to themselves.

The gibbons are tree-living apes but they find it easier than the orangs to travel through the branches because they are smaller. A gibbon swinging through the tree tops is one of the most glorious sights the tropical forest has to offer. It hurls itself 9 or 10 m across space, grabbing a branch and swinging itself off again in another dazzling swoop through the air. Its arms are as long as its legs and torso combined, so long that when it comes down to the ground, they cannot be used as props or crutches, but have to be held above its head, out of the way.

Because the gibbons are small, there is usually enough fruit on a tree to satisfy several of them, so it is practical for them to travel together and they live in tightly knit families. A pair is accompanied by up to four of their offspring of varying ages. Every morning, the family sings in chorus. In many ways they are like the indris of Madagascar. One creature uses its forelimbs to leap through the trees and the other its hind. Otherwise, the tropical rain forest in these different parts of the world has produced creatures that are remarkably similar – families of singing, vegetarian gymnasts.

The two African apes, unlike their Asian relations, live mostly on the ground. Gorillas live in central Africa. Young gorillas often climb trees, but they do so rather carefully and without the confidence of orangs. This is hardly surprising. The gorilla's foot cannot grasp in the way that an orang's can, so the arms provide the main means of hauling up the body. When gorillas descend, they do so feet-first. They lower themselves with their arms, and brake by pressing the soles of their feet flat on the trunk.

The big adult males are so huge, weighing up to 275 kg, that only the stoutest trees can support them. They climb rarely for they feed on vegetation that grows on the ground, such as nettles, bedstraw creeper and giant celery. Usually, they also sleep on the ground, making a bed among the flattened vegetation. They live in family groups of a dozen or so, each being led by a male. They sit quietly grazing, ripping huge handfuls of stems from the ground, lolling among the dense nettles and celery, sometimes grooming one another. For the most part they sit in silence. Occasionally they exchange quiet grunts or gurgles. While the adults doze, the young play and wrestle. Sometimes they rear up on their hind legs to beat a quick tattoo on their chests, practising the gesture the adults use in display. The male leads and protects his group. If he is frightened and

angered by intruders, he may roar and even charge. A blow from his fist can smash a human's bones. If he is pestered by a younger rival, he may fight. But the bulk of his days are spent quietly and in peace.

The calm nature of the gorilla is connected with its diet and what it has to do to get it. It lives entirely on vegetation of which there is an endless supply nearby. As it is so big and powerful it has no real enemies and there is no need for it to be nimble in either body or mind.

The other African ape, the chimpanzee, has a very different diet – and temperament. Whereas a gorilla may eat two dozen kinds of leaves and fruit, the chimpanzee feeds on 200 or so and in addition, termites, ants, honey, birds' eggs, birds and even small mammals like monkeys. To do this, it has to be both quick and inquisitive.

Chimpanzees are skilful climbers, sleeping and feeding in trees, but they travel and rest on the ground, even in thick forest. There they move on all fours, with their hands knuckles down and their long arms held stiffly. Even when the group is settled and at ease on the ground, there is constant activity. Youngsters chase one another up trees and play tag and king-of-the-castle.

African apes
The gorilla (*above*), the biggest of all living apes, spends most of its time on the ground when it is full grown. The chimpanzee (*below*), which is smaller, climbs trees readily throughout its life.

A life in the trees

Ape mothers and babies
Young chimpanzees stay with their mothers for the first five years of their lives and learn a great deal from them.

The sexual bonds between chimpanzees vary. Some females and some males only have one mate while others mate with many partners. The tie between the young and their mothers is always very close. Immediately after birth, the infant clings to its mother's hair with its tiny fists. It will remain close to its mother, riding on her back when the group travels, until it is about five years old. This close dependence has a great effect on chimpanzee society. The young learn a great deal from their mother and she is able to keep a close eye on them as they grow up, overseeing what they do, pulling them back from danger, showing them from her own example how to behave.

Chimpanzees are very inquisitive and this has probably led to their use of tools. When the group visits a termite hill, an animal will break off a twig and strip it of its leaves. It pokes the twig into one of the holes. When it pulls it out again, it is covered with soldier termites. The chimp draws the stem through its lips, taking off the insects and eating them. Chimps, in fact, not only use tools but make them.

So the early primates which had lived on the ground, moving usually at night and guided largely by their sense of smell, changed when they took to the trees. They became active by day, relied on their excellent eyesight and had hands for grasping instead of paws for running. With the aid of these talents, the monkeys and apes have made a great success of their life in the trees. But those of them that returned to the ground, whether it was because of increasing body size or some other reason, found that these very talents could be used in new ways. The enlarged brain led to an increase in learning and the beginnings of a group culture. The grasping hand and the coordinated eyes made possible the making and use of tools. The primates that are practising these skills today are repeating a process that another branch of their family started soon after the ancestral apes first appeared in Africa 20 million years ago. It was this branch that eventually stood upright and developed their talents to such a degree that they came to dominate the world in a way that no animal had ever done before.

13· The arrival of mankind

At home in the forest
Some people, like this boy with a blowpipe in the Amazonian jungle, can find in the forest all they need to keep alive. They gather wild fruit and vegetables, fish and hunt animals.

Mankind has suddenly become the most numerous of all large animals. 10,000 years ago, there were about 10 million human beings in the world. They were clever and communicative but their numbers seemed to be limited in much the same way as population of other animals are. Then, about 8000 years ago, their number began to increase rapidly. 2000 years ago it had risen to 300 million; and 1000 years ago, the species began to overrun the earth. Today, there are over 4000 million individuals. By the turn of the century there will be over 6000 million. These extraordinary creatures have spread to all corners of the earth. They live on the ice of the Poles and in the tropical jungles on the equator. They have climbed the highest mountains and dived down to walk on the bed of the sea. Some have even left the planet altogether and visited the moon.

Why did this happen? What power did mankind suddenly gain? The story starts 5 million years ago on the plains of Africa. The grass and scrub-covered landscape was then much as it is today. Some of the creatures that lived there were giant versions of modern species – a pig as big as a cow with tusks 1 m long, an immense buffalo, and an elephant standing a third again as tall as the one that is found there now. But others were very like species alive today – zebra, rhinoceros and giraffe. There were also several kinds of ape-like creatures about the size of chimpanzees. They were descendants of forest-living apes that had been widespread through not only Africa but Europe and Asia about 10 million years ago. All researchers are

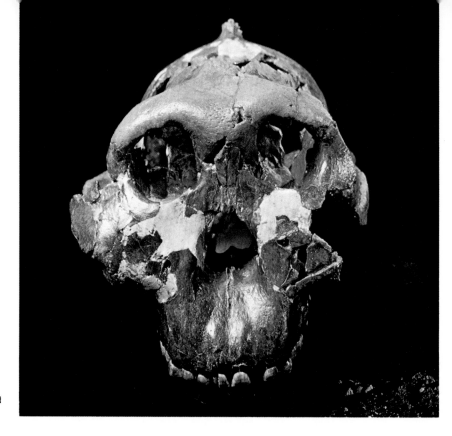

The skull of an ape-man
There were several different kinds
of ape-men in Africa. This one lived
about 2 million years ago.

agreed that among these creatures are the ancestors of modern human beings. As a group, they can be called ape-men.

They were not plentiful and their fossilized bones are rare, but enough have been found to give a fairly clear idea of what they were like in life. Their hands and feet resembled those of their tree-climbing ancestors and were very good at grasping things with nails on the fingers, not claws. The limbs were not so good for running as those of the antelopes or the carnivores. Their skulls also show signs of their forest-dwelling past. The eyes were well-developed and their sense of smell must have been poor. The teeth were small and rounded and not well-suited to grinding grass or tearing flesh. So what did these creatures eat out on the plain? They may have gathered roots, berries, nuts and fruit, but they also became hunters.

The structure of their hip bones shows that they began to stand upright around the time they moved onto the plains. The tree-living primates that used their hands for plucking fruit and leaves already had upright torsos. Many of these had also been able to stand up on their hind legs for short periods when they were on the ground. A permanent upright posture must have been very useful for a life on the plains. The ape-men were small, defenceless and slow, compared with the hunters of the plains, so advance warning of the approach of enemies must have been of the greatest importance. The ability to stand upright and look around might make the difference between life and death. It would also have been of great value in hunting. All the other hunters on the plain – lions, hunting dogs, hyenas – gather a great deal of information from smell. They keep their noses to the ground. But the ape-men's sense of smell was relatively poor. Sight was their most important sense, as it had been in the trees. They had more to gain from getting their heads high and looking into the distance than sniffing a patch of dusty grass.

An upright position is not a way of running faster. A highly-trained human athlete can barely maintain a speed of 25 km/h for any distance whereas monkeys, galloping on all fours, can go twice as fast. But standing on two legs does bring an advantage. The ape-men already had hands with a precise and powerful grip. If they stood upright, their hands could be ready at all times to make up for the lack of teeth and claws. If they were threatened by enemies, they could defend themselves by hurling stones and using sticks as clubs. They might not be able to tear open a dead animal with their teeth as a lion could do, but they could cut it open using the sharp edge of a stone, held in the hand. They could even take one stone, strike it against another and so shape it. Many such stones have been found beside the skeletons of ape-men. The creatures had become tool-makers. So ape-men claimed a permanent place for themselves among the inhabitants of the plains.

This situation lasted for about 3 million years. Slowly the bodies of one line of ape-men became better adapted to living on the plains. The feet became more suited to running, lost their ability to grasp and developed a slight arch. The hips changed to balance the upright torso, and the pelvis became broader to support the belly in its new upright position. The spine developed a slight curve so that the weight of the upper part of the body was better centred. Most importantly, the skull changed. The jaw became smaller and the forehead more domed. The brain of the first ape-men had been about the same size as that of a gorilla. Now it was double the size. And the animal grew to a height of a 1.5 m. Science has given this creature the name – Homo erectus or Upright Man.

These creatures were much more skilled toolmakers than their forerunners. Some of the stones they chipped were carefully shaped with a point at one end and sharp edge on either side and fitted neatly into the hand. Evidence of one of their successful hunts has been unearthed in southeast Kenya. In one small area lie the broken skeletons of giant baboons of a species that is now extinct. At least 50 adult animals and a dozen young appear to have been slaughtered here. Among their remains are hundreds of chipped stones and several thousand rough cobbles. All are made of rock that does not occur naturally within 30 km of the site. This find suggests several things. The way the stones have been chipped and shaped shows that the hunters were Upright Men. The fact that the stones come from a distant site suggests that the hunts were planned and that the hunters had armed themselves long before they found their prey. Baboons are fierce creatures with powerful fanged jaws. Few people today would be prepared to tackle them without firearms. The numbers killed at this one site suggests that such hunts were team operations demanding a great deal of skill.

Flint hand axes
These were made by Upright Man and were discovered in southeast England.

A flint arrowhead
Razor-sharp arrowheads were made from flint or volcanic glass throughout the last few thousand years in many parts of the world, from Australia to North America. This one was found in the Sahara.

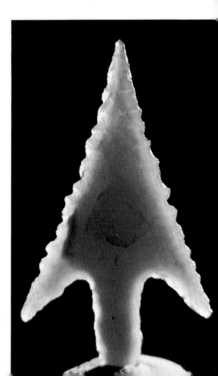

Biami men
The meaning of smiles and frowns is understood by all people everywhere.

We do not know if they used language to discuss their plans and carry out their attacks. However, they had another way of communicating – by gesture. Human beings have more separate muscles in their face than any other animal. So they can move the various parts of the face – lips, cheeks, forehead, eyebrows – in a great number of ways. There is little doubt that the face was the centre of early people's gestural communication.

One of the most important pieces of information the human face passes on is identity. We take it for granted that all our faces are very different from one another, yet this is very unusual among animals. If individuals are to cooperate in a team, then they must be able to tell one from another. Many social animals, such as hyenas and wolves, do this by smell. Human beings' sense of smell, however, was much less sensitive than their sight, so their identities were made clear by the shape of the face.

Since the features of the face can be moved, they can reveal a great deal of information about moods and intentions. We have little difficulty in understanding expressions of enthusiasm, delight, disgust, anger and amusement. But quite apart from such feelings, we also send messages with our faces – of agreement and disagreement, of welcome and invitation. Are the gestures we use today ones that we have learned from our parents and share with the rest of the community because we have the same social background? Or are they an inheritance from our prehistoric past? Some gestures, such as ways of counting or insulting, vary from society to society and are clearly learned. But others appear to be more universal. Did early people, for example, nod agreement and shake their heads in disapproval as we do? Clues to the answers can come from the gestures used by people from another society who have had no contact whatever with our own.

New Guinea is one of the last places in the world where such people might be found. Ten years ago I was there with an expedition looking for people of the Biami tribe who had never seen Europeans before. One morning, we awoke to find seven of them standing in the bush nearby. As we scrambled out of our tents, they stood their ground. It was an act of great trust and we tried to show that we were friendly. We spoke to them, but the Biami understood nothing. We had to rely entirely on such gestures as we had in common, and it turned out that there were many of them. We smiled – and the Biami smiled back. The gesture may seem an odd one as a sign of friendliness, for it draws attention to the teeth which are the only natural weapon that human beings have. The important part, however, is not the teeth but the movement of the lips. In other primates, this is a gesture of peace-making. Among humans the gesture has changed by upturning the ends of the mouth and is used to show welcome and pleasure. We can be sure that this expression has not been learned entirely from our parents, because even babies that are born deaf and blind will smile when they are picked up to be fed.

We had brought goods to trade with the Biami – beads, salt, knives, cloth. We pointed to the net bag one of them held and raised our eyebrows questioningly. The Biami understood immediately and pulled out taro roots and some green bananas. We began to trade. Pointing at an object, touching fingers to show numbers, nodding our heads in agreement; all these gestures were clear. We all used our eyebrows a great deal. They are the most movable features of the face and their main use must be for signalling. The Biami drew their eyebrows together to show disapproval. When they accompanied this by shaking their heads, they made it clear that they did not want the beads that we offered. By raising their eyebrows when they examined our knives, they showed wonder. When I caught the glance of a man standing at one side of the group and raised my eyebrows at the same time as giving a slight backward jerk of my head, the Biami man did the same. This gesture seems to be a way of showing that each of us knew the other was there – and was happy that he should be.

Biami meet Europeans
Some signs are the individual inventions of different groups. This Biami man is explaining how many rivers there are in his country. Touching each finger represents to his people a particular number – tapping the elbow means eight, touching the neck means eleven.

The arrival of mankind

This eyebrow flash is used all over the world. The fact that this and several other signals are so widespread suggests that they are a common inheritance. They may well have been used by early people as they planned their hunts, greeted friends, worked together to catch prey and brought it back to the delight of their mates and children.

With this improved talent for communication and skill in making tools, early people became more and more successful. From southeastern Africa they moved into the Nile valley and northwards to the eastern shores of the Mediterranean. Their remains have been found farther east in Java and in China. Whether they migrated into Asia from Africa or whether the people whose remains have been found there were the descendants of an Asiatic ape-man we still do not know. Some of the African groups also reached Europe.

Upright Man arrived in Europe about a million years ago. But about 600,000 years ago the climate changed. It started to get very cold. The sea level lowered so that there was land between some of the continents and islands. Now people spread into the Americas across the Bering Strait and down the island chains of Indonesia towards New Guinea and Australia.

In Europe, these early people must have felt the increasing cold very keenly. They had developed in the warmth of the African plain

A bushman hunting party
The bushmen of southwestern Africa grow no crops and keep no domestic animals except dogs. They may spend many days tracking one particular creature, such as a giraffe, before they bring it down with poisoned arrows and spears.

and did not have the protection of thick fur. Most creatures facing such a problem would have moved to warmer parts or simply died out. These people, being inventive and skilful with their hands, did neither. They hunted the furry animals, stripped the skins from the dead bodies and used them themselves. And they found shelter in caves.

Their living sites have been discovered in great numbers in caves in southern France and Spain. From the objects that have been found in them, we know a great deal about these people. They used bone needles to sew clothes of skin and fur. They fished with carefully carved bone harpoons and hunted with spears tipped with stone blades. Blackened stones show that they had control of fire which gave them warmth in the winter. It also enabled them to cook the meat that their small teeth could not otherwise have chewed.

Their teeth had become even smaller than those of their ancestors, but their skulls had grown and were now as big as our own. The part of the brain that controls speech was fully developed, so we can assume that these people now spoke complex language. There is no important difference between the skeletons of the people who lived in the caves of France 35,000 years ago and ours. Scientists have given them the same name as they use for all modern humans – Homo sapiens, or Wise Man.

Jungle wealth
The Amazon tribes are expert at using the riches of the forest. A tree trunk, hollowed out with fire and, until quite recently, with axes of stone, makes an excellent canoe (*above*). The headdresses they wear for their complex dance rituals (*below*) are made from the feathers of parrots and macaws. The juice of berries provides paint for their bodies and the flutes, with which they make music, are cut from bamboo.

The arrival of mankind

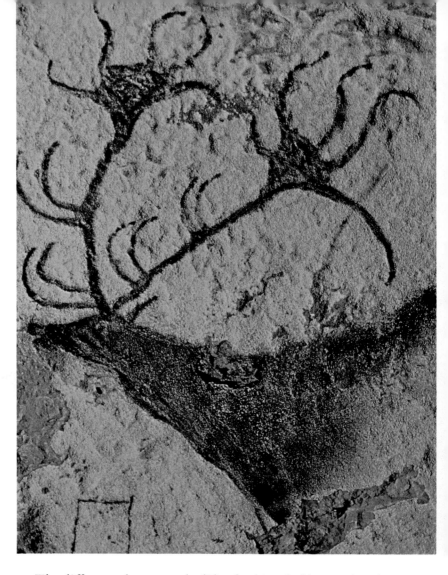

A prehistoric animal portrait
This magnificently antlered stag was painted on the walls of a cave at Lascaux in France about 15000 years ago. The square beneath it was drawn about the same time but its meaning is a mystery.

The difference between the life of a skin-clad hunter leaving a cave with a spear over his shoulder to hunt mammoth, and a smartly dressed executive driving along a motorway in New York, London or Tokyo to consult his computer print-out, is not due to any further physical development of body or brain, but to something completely new.

Once we thought that the difference between humans and animals was that we were the only creatures to make and use tools. We now know that this is not so. Chimpanzees and some other animals do so. Even our complex spoken language seems less special the more we learn about the communications used by chimpanzees and dolphins. But we are the only creatures to have painted pictures showing real objects. It is this talent which in the end transformed the life of mankind.

Its first flowering can be seen in those ancient European caves. There, in some of the most remote parts of the caverns, people painted designs on the walls. For colour they used the red, brown and yellow of iron, and black from charcoal. For brushes, they used

sticks, their fingers, and sometimes blew paint on the rock from their mouths. Their subjects were almost always the animals they hunted – mammoth, deer, horse, wild cattle, bison and rhinoceros. Often they were painted or scratched one on top of the other. There were no landscapes and only very rarely human figures. In one or two caves, the people left stencilled outlines of their hands. Scattered among the animals, there were abstract designs – lines, squares, grids, rows of dots, curves and chevrons that might be arrows. These were the least spectacular of the designs but the most important for what was to come.

We do not know why these people painted. Perhaps the designs were part of a religious ritual. If the chevrons surrounding a great bull represented arrows, then maybe they were drawn to bring success in hunting. If the cattle shown with swollen sides were meant to be pregnant, then maybe they were made during fertility rituals. Or perhaps the people painted simply because they enjoyed doing so. But whether the paintings were directed at the gods or other people, they were certainly communications.

Hunting magic ?
Animals that provided the people with food are sometimes shown in the prehistoric caves with arrow-like shapes drawn on them, like this bison in a cave at Niaux in France. It may be that the arrows do represent weapons and that the act of drawing them was part of a ritual to bring success in hunting bison, but no one can be sure.

The arrival of mankind

Today it is still possible to discover what purposes rock painting can have to a hunting people. In Australia, the Aborigines draw designs on rock that are very similar to the prehistoric designs of Europe. They are painted on cliffs and rock shelters, often in places that are extremely difficult to reach. They are painted with colours from minerals and often they are one on top of another. They include geometrical designs and stencilled handprints and very often they show creatures on which the Aborigines rely for food – barramundi fish, turtles, lizards and kangaroo. Some designs are repainted time and time again, in the belief that by keeping the image fresh on the rock the animals they represent will continue to flourish in the bush.

The Aborigines are no more closely related to the prehistoric cave dwellers of France than we are, but their traditional way of life is still close to that of the Stone Age. Homo sapiens led such a life, hunting animals and gathering fruits, seeds and roots everywhere in the world for many thousands of years. Such a life is dangerous and rough. Those individuals whose bodies were better suited to the conditions had an advantage. So they survived and reproduced, handing on that advantage to their children.

Rock painting today
The Walbiri people of central Australia believe that this cliff in their territory is the home of a great snake god which took part, with other spirits, in the creation of the world. Its image is painted on the rock and men came to place their own symbols beside it (*below*) and then worship beneath it (*below opposite*).

An x-ray fish
In some parts of Australia, the Aborigines paint the animals they hunt, such as this barramundi fish, on special rocks. They show it, not just as they see it but as they know it to be, complete with bones, muscles and internal organs.

The arrival of mankind

The end of a hunt
An Aboriginal man returns with a wallaby which he killed with a spear launched from the spearthrower he carries in his left hand.

So the bodies of human beings responded to the world they lived in. Those that lived in the tropics, like the Australian Aborigines and the Africans, had dark skins. Dark skin colour may have developed separately in many different places so a black skin is not by itself proof of a close relationship to another black skin. Its purpose is protection. The rays of the sun can cause cancer on unprotected fair skin. Dark skin colour, however, provides a shield. Many people living in hot places, in Africa, India and Australia, also have long, thin bodies. This shape helps keep the body cool in hot, dry surroundings. In cold areas, the situation is reversed. Some sun is important for good health. So in the north, where the sun is so often hidden, people like the Lapps of Scandinavia have fair skins. The Eskimos, living within the Arctic Circle, also have a light-coloured skin and a body type that is the opposite of the gangling desert-dweller. They are short and squat, which is the shape which best holds heat.

People who live by hunting and gathering still exist. The Aborigines and the African bushmen live in deserts. Other groups

A Lapp and his reindeer
The Lapps rely on reindeer for their meat, milk and clothes. Although they harness some of the deer to their sledges, they cannot lead the whole herd just where they want. Instead the people have to follow the reindeer as the herd moves over the bleak land in search of grass and moss during the harsh northern winter.

find all they need from the rain forests in central Africa and Malaysia. They all live in harmony with the natural world around them, not changing it and making do with what it provides. Nowhere are they very numerous. They do not live long and many children do not survive because of the scarcity of food and other dangers. Such has been the condition of our species for almost all the million years that it has existed.

Then, about 8000 years ago, the human population began to increase. The trigger may have been a wild grass that grew on the sandy hills and fertile river banks of the Middle East. It bears lots of nourishing seeds that are easily plucked and separated from their husks. Doubtless people had gathered it and eaten it whenever they came across it. But a change came when they realized that if they planted some of the seeds that they gathered, they would no longer have to search for the plant the following summer. They could stop wandering and become farmers. They could build themselves permanent huts and live in villages. So they founded the first towns.

The arrival of mankind

The earliest writing
This tablet of baked clay was found in the ruins of the city of Uruk in Iraq. It is about 5000 years old.

The inheritors of abilities produced by a new kind of change – cultural evolution

Uruk, in Iraq, was built on what was then the marshy delta between the Tigris and Euphrates Rivers. Now it is a desert. The town was a complex one. The people planted fields of grain around it and kept herds of goats and sheep. They made pottery. This settled life enabled them to make an important advance in communication. People who travel all the time cannot have many possessions but people who live in houses can do so. In the remains of one of the buildings at Uruk the earliest known piece of writing has been found. It is a small clay tablet, covered with marks. No one yet knows exactly what it means. The marks are simple diagrams but ones that must have been recognized by the people for whom they were meant.

When people baked that tablet they changed the course of evolution. Now individuals could pass on information to others without being there. People in other parts of the world and in future generations could now learn from them. Other people elsewhere, in the valley of the Nile, the jungles of central America and the plains of China, made the same discoveries. Pictures of objects became simplified and took on new meanings. Some came to represent simply sounds. At the eastern end of the Mediterranean, people developed them into a system in which every sound they spoke had a shape that could be cut in stone, scored on clay or drawn on paper. So writing was developed. The revolution based on the sharing of experience and the spread of knowledge had begun. Later, the development of printing spread this knowledge even further. Today, our libraries can be seen as huge communal brains, memorizing far more than any one human brain could hold. It is this stored knowledge that enables us to find ways of controlling our environment. Our knowledge of agriculture and machines, of medicine and engineering, of mathematics and space travel, all depend on stored experience. Cut off from our libraries and all they represent and marooned on a desert island, any one of us would be quickly reduced to the life of a hunter-gatherer.

This last chapter has dealt with only one species, ourselves. This may have given the impression that human beings are the final triumph of evolution and that all these millions of years of development of animals and plant life have had no purpose other than to put us on earth. There is no scientific evidence whatever to support such a view. There is no reason to suppose that our stay here will be any more permanent than that of the dinosaur. The processes of evolution are still going on among plants and birds, insects and mammals. So it is more than likely that if humans were to disappear from the face of the earth, there is a creature somewhere that would develop into a new form and take our place.

Denying that we have a special position in the natural world might seem modest, but it might also be used as an excuse for avoiding our responsibilities. The fact is that no species has ever had such control over the earth as we now have. That lays a huge responsibility upon us. It is not only our own future that lies in our hands, but that of all other living creatures with whom we share the earth.

Acknowledgements

This book is based on a series of programmes made for BBC Television called *Life on Earth*. The series took three years to make. One way or another, nearly a hundred people contributed to it. With such a large team, it is very difficult to sort out who contributed what. Cameramen, after many hours of patient waiting and watching, captured a particular action of an animal that had never been described before and made the rest of us (as well as tens of millions of television viewers) feel we had actually seen it for ourselves. Sound recordists listened to my words as I tried to explain something – and made me think again if I was not being clear. Researchers discovered descriptions of little-known animals that illustrated my points in a better and more unusual way than the examples I had first thought of. Scientists, who had researched for years on particular animals, most generously told us of their discoveries and made it possible for us to film the creatures that they had come to know so intimately. Most important of all, for me, the three producers of the films, Richard Brock, Christopher Parsons and John Sparks, helped with great skill and imagination to shape the programmes. While the films were being made, I was also writing the book of the series. Inevitably, the contributions of the film team were reflected in what I wrote. So I am greatly indebted to all of them.

After the *Life on Earth* book had been published, it was suggested that a version should be produced that had many less words and many more pictures. This is it. Ingrid Selberg laboured hard to simplify my original sentences and make my narrative clearer. Enid Fairhead, helped by Caroline Hill and Diane Rich, produced this splendid new set of illustrations and designed the layout of the pages. To them, *Discovering Life on Earth* owes its existence and I am very grateful indeed to them.

Index

Index

Index

Picture credits

The credits for each page read from left to right in strict descending sequence. Where all photographs on one page come from the same source the credit is given once only.

The reconstructions of prehistoric life were first published in the augmented and enlarged edition of LIFE ON EARTH, and are Copyright © 1980 The Reader's Digest Association Limited, London.

Front cover M.P.L. Fogden/Bruce Coleman Ltd. **Back cover** John Sparks.

1 The endless variety

9 David Attenborough: Tui A. de Roy/Bruce Coleman Inc. 10 Maurice Tibbles/Wildlife Picture Agency. 11 David Attenborough. 12–13 Adrian Deere-Jones/Bruce Coleman Ltd. 14 Chaumeton/Jacana: Gene Cox/Bruce Coleman Ltd: David Attenborough. 15 Heather Angel. 16 Paul Brierley: Kim Taylor/Bruce Coleman Ltd. 17 David Attenborough. 18 Kim Taylor/Bruce Coleman Ltd: Tom Stack/Tom Stack & Associates: Tom Stack/Tom Stack & Associates. 19 Peter Parks/Oxford Scientific Films. 20 Kim Taylor/Bruce Coleman Ltd. 21 Steve Small/Tom Stack & Associates: Christian Petron/Seaphot: Peter Capen/Seaphot: David Hill/Natural Science Photos. 22 Frieder Sauer/Bruce Coleman Ltd: Kenneth Lucas/Seaphot. 23 D.P. Wilson/Eric and David Hosking: W.M. Stephens/Tom Stack & Associates: Valerie Taylor/Ardea London. 24 Peter Scoones/Seaphot: D.P. Wilson/Eric and David Hosking: Woody Pridgen/Vision International: Chaumeton/Nature. 25 Neville Coleman/Bruce Coleman Ltd: David Attenborough. 26 Woody Pridgen/Vision International: Peter Scoones/Seaphot: Valerie Taylor/Ardea London.

2 Building bodies

27 Chaumeton/Nature: Lanceau/Nature. 28 Peter Parks/Oxford Scientific Films: Christian Petron/Seaphot: Valerie Taylor/Ardea London. 29 Isobel Bennett/Natural Science Photos: Kenneth Lucas/Seaphot. 30 Christian Petron/Seaphot: Peter Parks/Oxford Scientific Films: Heather Angel/Z. Leszczynski/Animals Animals/Oxford Scientific Films. 31 Artist, Tom Adams. 32 Chaumeton/Nature: Valerie Taylor/Ardea London: Jane Burton/Bruce Coleman Ltd. 33 Laboute/Jacana: James Carmichael/N.H.P.A. 34 Jane Burton/Bruce Coleman Ltd: Chaumeton/Nature. 35 David George/Seaphot: Peter David/Seaphot. 36 Jane Burton/Bruce Coleman Ltd: Pat Morris/Ardea London: Chaumeton/Jacana: Neville Coleman/Bruce Coleman Ltd. 37 Chaumeton/Nature: Chaumeton/Nature: Walter Deas/Seaphot: Pecolatto/Jacana: Walter Deas/Seaphot: Ken Lucas/Seaphot: Jane Burton/Bruce Coleman Ltd. 38 Jane Burton/Bruce Coleman Ltd: Valerie Taylor/Ardea London: Paul Brierley: Chaumeton/Nature. 39 David Attenborough. 40 Inigo Everson/Bruce Coleman Ltd: Jane Burton/Bruce Coleman Ltd: Tom McHugh/National Audubon Society Collection/Photo Researchers: Tom McHugh/National Audubon Society Collection/Photo Researchers. 41 Tom McHugh/National Audubon Society Collection/Photo Researchers: Christian Petron/Seaphot. 42 Ed Ross: Ed Ross: A. Hutson/Natural Science Photos.

3 The first forests

43 Gerald Cubitt/Bruce Coleman Ltd: Hans Reinhard/Bruce Coleman Ltd: G.J. Cambridge/N.H.P.A.: G.J. Cambridge/N.H.P.A. 44 Jane Burton/Bruce Coleman Ltd: Peter Ward/Bruce Coleman Ltd: M.P.L. Fogden/Bruce Coleman Ltd. 45 Moiton/Jacana: Ian Beames/Ardea London. 46 Robert Mitchell/Tom Stack & Associates: Anthony Bannister/N.H.P.A. 47 K.G. Preston-Mafham/Premaphotos Wildlife: S.C. Bisserot/Bruce Coleman Ltd: Jane Burton/Bruce Coleman Ltd: Lorne/Jacana. 48–49 Artist: Tom Adams. 50 Jean-Paul Ferrero/Nature: John Mason/Ardea London: Bob Gibbons/Ardea London. 51 G.I. Bernard/Oxford Scientific Films: Heather Angel: John Mason/Ardea London. 52 Stephen Dalton/N.H.P.A.: Schrempp/Frank Lane: Peter Parks/Oxford Scientific Films. 53 Stephen Dalton/N.H.P.A.: Rouxaime/Jacana: Gunter Ziesler: K.G. Preston-Mafham/Premaphotos Wildlife.

54 K.G. Preston-Mafham/Premaphotos Wildlife: Stephen Dalton/Bruce Coleman Ltd: G.E. Hyde. 55 Jane Burton/Bruce Coleman Ltd: Davidson/Frank Lane: Stephen Dalton/N.H.P.A.: Lennart Norstrom. 56 Hans Reinhard/Bruce Coleman Ltd: K.G. Preston-Mafham/Premaphotos Wildlife: K.G. Preston-Mafham/N.H.P.A. 57 Duerden/Frank Lane: Prato 50341/Bruce Coleman Ltd: Hans Reinhard/Bruce Coleman Ltd: Heather Angel: Heather Angel. 58 Dr.J.A.L. Cooke/Oxford Scientific Films: Robert Mitchell/Tom Stack & Associates: Robert Mitchell/Tom Stack & Associates.

4 Insect armies

59 Gunter Ziesler: Ed Ross: Gunter Ziesler: Heather Angel. 60–61 Artist: Peter Barrett. 62 Central Sequence: Lanceau/Nature: F. Greenaway/N.H.P.A. 63 Jane Burton/Bruce Coleman Ltd: Chaumeton/Nature: Ed Ross: Heather Angel: Anthony Healy/Bruce Coleman Ltd: Eisebeiss/Frank Lane. 64 Paul Brierley: Gunter Ziesler: Peter Ward/Bruce Coleman Ltd: Alan Weaving/Ardea London: E. Burgess/Ardea London: Ed Ross. 65 Sequence top left: Moiton/Jacana: Prato 20.442/Bruce Coleman Ltd. 66 Lanceau/Nature: Raymond A. Mendez/Animals Animals/Oxford Scientific Films: Ed Ross: Ian Beames/Ardea London. 67 Stephen Dalton/Bruce Coleman Ltd: Gunter Ziesler: Chaumeton/Nature: M.P.L. Fogden/Bruce Coleman Ltd. 68 Ed Ross: Heather Angel: Carol Hughes/Bruce Coleman Ltd: Stephen Dalton/Bruce Coleman Ltd: Chaumeton/Jacana. 69 Stephen Dalton/N.H.P.A.: Queensland Museum/Natural Science Photos: Anthony Bannister/N.H.P.A.: P.H. & S.L. Ward/Natural Science Photos. 70 Ed Ross: Anthony Bannister/N.H.P.A.: Jean-Paul Ferrero/Ardea London. 71 Chaumeton/Nature: Ian Beames/Ardea London: Ed Ross. 72 Colin G. Butler/Bruce Coleman Ltd: Stephen Dalton/N.H.P.A.: Stephen Dalton/N.H.P.A.: Prato 50660/Bruce Coleman Ltd: Lanceau/Nature: John Mason/Ardea London: John Mason/Ardea London. 73 Ed Ross: Gunter Ziesler: Ed Ross: D. Yendall/Natural Science Photos: G.H. Thompson/Oxford Scientific Films. 74 Ed Ross: A.J. Deane/Bruce Coleman Ltd: K.G. Preston-Mafham/Premaphotos Wildlife: Rod Borland/Bruce Coleman Ltd: Ed Ross.

5 The conquest of the waters

75 Chaumeton/Nature. 76 Tom Stack/Tom Stack & Associates: Russ Kinne/National Audubon Society Collection/Photo Researchers. 77 Roger Miles/British Museum (N.H.) 78–79 Artist: Peter Barrett. 80 Ed Robinson/Tom Stack & Associates: Valerie Taylor/Ardea London: Dick Clarke/Seaphot. 81 Walter Deas/Seaphot: Peter Parks/Oxford Scientific Films: M. Timothy O'Keefe/Bruce Coleman Ltd: John Paling/Oxford Scientific Films. 82 Chaumeton/Nature: D.P. Wilson/Eric and David Hosking. 83 Chaumeton/Nature: Jane Burton/Bruce Coleman Ltd. 84 Neville Coleman/Bruce Coleman Ltd: Chaumeton/Nature: Varin-Visage/Jacana: Allan Power/Bruce Coleman Ltd. 85 Pecolatto/Jacana: Carl Roessler/Animals Animals/Oxford Scientific Films. 86 Jane Burton/Bruce Coleman Ltd: André Roth/British Museum (N.H.) 87 R.H. Johnson/Seaphot: Z. Leszczynski/Animals Animals/Oxford Scientific Films: Kenneth Lucas/Seaphot: Pecolatto/Jacana: Soames Summerhays/Biofotos: Z. Leszczynski/Animals Animals/Oxford Scientific Films. 88 Bassot/Nature: Peter David/Seaphot: Peter Parks/Oxford Scientific Films. 89 Bassot/Nature: Hans Reinhard/Bruce Coleman Ltd: Peter Parks/Oxford Scientific Films. 90 Dale Johnson/Tom Stack & Associates: Jeff Foott/Bruce Coleman Ltd: Dan Guravich/National Audubon Society Collection/Photo Researchers.

6 The invasion of the land

91 Pat Morris/Ardea London: Peter Scoones/Seaphot. 92 Tom McHugh/National Audubon Society Collection/Photo Researchers: Bruce Coleman Ltd. 93 Artist: Peter Barrett. 94 Ken Brate/National Audubon Society Collection/Photo Researchers: Jane Burton/Bruce Coleman Ltd: Heather Angel. 95 Jane Burton/Bruce Coleman Ltd. 96 Tom McHugh/National Audubon Society Collection/Photo Researchers: Stephen Dalton/N.H.P.A.: Adrian Warren/Ardea London: Adrian Warren/Ardea London. 97 Jan Taylor/Bruce Coleman Ltd: Ron Dillow/Tom Stack & Associates: M.P.L. Fogden/Bruce Coleman Ltd: Heather Angel. 98 Pat Morris/Ardea London: Jane Burton/Bruce Coleman Ltd: Heather Angel: M.P.L. Fogden/Bruce Coleman Ltd. 99 M.P.L. Fogden/Bruce Coleman Ltd: Jane Burton/Bruce Coleman Ltd: Kenneth Lucas/Seaphot: Gunter Ziesler: Heather Angel. 100 Kim Taylor/Bruce Coleman Ltd. 101 Lanceau/Nature: Eric Lindgren/Ardea London. 102 G.I. Bernard/Oxford Scientific Films: Stephen Dalton/N.H.P.A.: Jane Burton/Bruce Coleman Ltd: Stephen Dalton/N.H.P.A.: Stephen Dalton/N.H.P.A.: Stephen Dalton/N.H.P.A. 103 G.I. Bernard/

Oxford Scientific Films: G.I. Bernard/Oxford Scientific Films: G.I. Bernard/Oxford Scientific Films: Stephen Dalton/N.H.P.A.: Stephen Dalton/N.H.P.A.: Stephen Dalton/N.H.P.A.: G.I. Bernard/Oxford Scientific Films: Stephen Dalton/N.H.P.A. 104 C. Mattison/Natural Science Photos: Ed Ross. 105 Lanceau/Nature: Devez/Jacana. 106 Ed Ross.

7 A watertight skin
107 Gunter Ziesler: Eric and David Hosking: Alan Root/Bruce Coleman Ltd.: A. Nelson/Tom Stack & Associates. 108 Rod Salm/Seaphot: Leonard Lee Rue 111/Tom Stack & Associates. 109 Heather Angel. 110–111 Artist: Charles Raymond. 112 Linden Bird. 113 Jeffrey W. Lang/National Audubon Society Collection/Photo Researchers: Jeffrey W. Lang/National Audubon Society Collection/Photo Researchers: Varin-Visage/Jacana. 114 Jonathan Blair/Susan Griggs Agency: Gerald Cubitt/Bruce Coleman Ltd. 115 Valerie Taylor/Ardea London: Walter Deas/Seaphot: Walter Deas/Seaphot: Walter Deas/Seaphot: Jack Egan/Tom Stack & Associates: Bill Wood/Seaphot. 116 C. Mattison/Natural Science Photos: C. Mattison/Natural Science Photos: M.P.L. Fogden/Bruce Coleman Ltd: Anthony Bannister/N.H.P.A. 117 Ferrero/Nature: Varin-Visage/Jacana: Z. Leszczynski/Animals Animals/Oxford Scientific Films: Eric and David Hosking. 118 Chaumeton/Nature: Jane Burton/Bruce Coleman Ltd: Heather Angel: Kim Taylor/Bruce Coleman Ltd: Stephen Dalton/Oxford Scientific Films: Kim Taylor/Bruce Coleman Ltd. 119 D.C. Rentz/Natural Science Photos: Robert Maier/Vision International: Ed Ross: Sean McKeown/Tom Stack & Associates. 120 Jean-Paul Ferrero/Ardea London: C.B. Frith/Bruce Coleman Ltd: Gunter Ziesler: C.H. McDougal/Ardea London. 121 Anthony Bannister/N.H.P.A.: Tom McHugh/National Audubon Society Collection/Photo Researchers: Ed Ross: Volot/Jacana. 122 Pat Morris/Ardea London: Stephen Dalton/Oxford Scientific Films: Varin-Visage/Jacana.

8 Lords of the air
123 David Thompson/Oxford Scientific Films: Jane Burton/Bruce Coleman Ltd. 124 Lanceau/Nature: Museum für Naturkunde, Berlin, GDR. 125 Jan Lindblad/National Audubon Society Collection/Photo Researchers. 126 Jeff Foott/Bruce Coleman Ltd: Wilhelm Möller/Ardea London: Boris/Nature: Hans Reinhard/Bruce Coleman Ltd: Ivan Polunin/N.H.P.A. 127 Dr.E.R. Degginger FPSA/Bruce Coleman Inc: Gunter Ziesler: R.J. Erwin/N.H.P.A. 128 Rod Salm/Seaphot. 129 Christian Zuber/Bruce Coleman Ltd: Kenneth Fink/Ardea London: David Hughes/Bruce Coleman Ltd: Kenneth Fink/Ardea London. 130 Gunter Ziesler: Bob and Clara Calhoun/Bruce Coleman Ltd. 131 Eric and David Hosking: Gunter Ziesler: Eric and David Hosking: Hugh Maynard/Bruce Coleman Ltd. 132 Gordon Lansbury/Bruce Coleman Ltd: Eric and David Hosking. 133 Robin Fletcher/Vision International: Bruce Coleman/Bruce Coleman Ltd: Francisco Erize/Bruce Coleman Inc: Gordon Lansbury/Bruce Coleman Ltd. 134 Gunter Ziesler: Tom McHugh/National Audubon Society Collection/Photo Researchers: Brian J. Coates/Bruce Coleman Inc. Brian J. Coates/Bruce Coleman Ltd. 135 Robinson/Frank Lane. 136 Gunter Ziesler: Tom McHugh/National Audubon Society Collection/Photo Researchers: Gunter Ziesler. 137 Jen and Des Bartlett/Bruce Coleman Inc: Gunter Ziesler. 138 Kenneth Fink/Ardea London.

9 Eggs, pouches and placentas
139 Tom McHugh/National Audubon Society Collection/Photo Researchers. 140 Dr.J.A.L. Cooke/Oxford Scientific Films. 141 Brian J. Coates/Bruce Coleman Inc: Bruce Coleman/Bruce Coleman Ltd. 142 Artist: Peter Barrett. 143 Bruce M. Wellman/Tom Stack & Associates. 144 Leonard Lee Rue 111/National Audubon Society/Photo Researchers: Leonard Lee Rue 111/Tom Stack & Associates. 145 C.C. Lockwood/Bruce Coleman Inc: Jack Dermid/Bruce Coleman Inc. 146 Graham Pizzey/Bruce Coleman Inc. 147 Warren Garst/Tom Stack & Associates. 148 Stanley Breeden: Fred J. Alsop/Bruce Coleman Inc. 149 Ferrero/Nature. 150 Hans and Judy Beste/Ardea London: Sean Morris/Oxford Scientific Films: Hans and Judy Beste/Ardea London: Ferrero/Nature. 151 Ferrero/Nature. 152 Eric Lindgren/National Audubon Society Collection/Photo Researchers. 153 Tom McHugh/National Audubon Society Collection/Photo Researchers. 154 Jacana.

10 Insect-eaters and others
155 Rod Williams/Bruce Coleman Ltd. 156 Jane Burton/Bruce Coleman Ltd: A & E Bomford/Ardea London: Dr.J.A.L. Cooke/Oxford Scientific Films. 157 Jane Burton/Bruce Coleman Ltd: Wardene Weisser/Ardea London. 158 Hans Reinhard/Bruce Coleman Ltd: Heather Angel. 159 Jane Burton/Bruce Coleman Ltd: Russ Kinne/National Audubon Society Collection/Photo Researchers. 160 D.H. Thompson/Oxford Scientific Films: Heather Angel. 161 Gerard/Jacana. 162 Dave Norris/National Audubon Society Collection/Photo Researchers: Jen and Des Bartlett/Bruce Coleman Ltd. 163 Michael Freeman/Bruce Coleman Ltd: Gohier/Nature: Breck P. Kent/Animals Animals/Oxford Scientific Films. 164 Peter Ward/Bruce Coleman Ltd: Tony Beamish/Ardea London. 165 George Holton/National Audubon Society Collection/Photo Researchers: Noel Speechley: Jane Burton/Bruce Coleman Ltd: Roy P. Fontaine/National Audubon Society Collection/Photo Researchers. 166 Nina Leen/Life/© Time Inc. 1966/Colorific: Russ Kinne/National Audubon Society Collection/Photo Researchers: L. Hugh Newman/N.H.P.A. 167 Jean-Philippe Varin/Jacana: Adrian Warren/Ardea London: Gunter Ziesler. 168 George Laycock/Bruce Coleman Ltd: Al Giddings/Ocean Films, Ltd. 169 Tom Stack/Tom Stack & Associates: Al Giddings/Ocean Films, Ltd: Gordon Williamson/Bruce Coleman Ltd. 170 Jane Burton/Bruce Coleman Ltd: Gohier/Ardea London.

11 The hunters and the hunted
171 G.I. Bernard/Oxford Scientific Films. 172 Jane Burton/Bruce Coleman Ltd. 173 Mark N. Boulton/National Audubon Society Collection/Photo Researchers: Kim Taylor/Bruce Coleman Ltd. 174 David C. Houston/Bruce Coleman Inc. 175 Tom McHugh/National Audubon Society Collection/Photo Researchers. 176 Gunter Ziesler: R. Van Nostrand/National Audubon Society Collection/Photo Researchers: G. Kinns/Natural Science Photos. 177 Hans Reinhard/Bruce Coleman Ltd. 178 Ed Ross: Ian Beames/Ardea London. 179 Tom Brakefield/Bruce Coleman Inc: Tom McHugh/National Audubon Society Collection/Photo Researchers. 180 Peter Johnson/N.H.P.A. 181 M. Philip Kahl/National Audubon Society Collection/Photo Researchers: David Cayleff/Wildlife Picture Agency. 182–183 Tex Fuller/Animals Animals/Oxford Scientific Films. 182 M.P. Kahl/Bruce Coleman Ltd. 183 Carol Hughes/Bruce Coleman Inc. 184 Hartman/Frank Lane: Warren Garst/Tom Stack & Associates. 185 Eric and David Hosking. 186 Sulvio Fresco/Bruce Coleman Inc.

12 A life in the trees
187 Rod Williams/Bruce Coleman Ltd. 188 Jean-Philippe Varin/Jacana. 189 Norman Myers/Bruce Coleman Inc. A. & E. Bomford/Ardea London. 190 A. & E. Bomford/Ardea London. 191 Tom McHugh/National Audubon Society Collection/Photo Researchers: Francisco Futil/Bruce Coleman Ltd: Devez/Jacana: Howard Uible/National Audubon Society Collection/Photo Researchers: S.C. Bisserot/Bruce Coleman Inc.: P. Morris/Ardea London. 192 Tony Beamish/Ardea London. 193 Jean-Philippe Varin/Jacana: Rod Williams/Bruce Coleman Ltd. 194 Varin-Visage/Jacana. 195 Tom McHugh/National Audubon Society Collection/Photo Researchers: Gary Milburn/Tom Stack & Associates. 196 S. Nagendra/National Audubon Society Collection/Photo Researchers: Tom McHugh/National Audubon Society Collection/Photo Researchers: Bruce Coleman/Bruce Coleman Ltd. 197 Akira Uchiyama/National Audubon Society Collection/Photo Researchers. 198 E. Hanumantha Rao/National Audubon Society Collection/Photo Researchers: David Attenborough. 199 Jean-Philippe Varin/Jacana. 200 J. Hobday/Natural Science Photos. 201 David Attenborough: Jean-Phillipe Varin/Jacana. 202 David Attenborough: John Sparks/N.H.P.A.

13 The arrival of mankind
203 John Wright/Alan Hutchison. 204 John Reader. 205 John Fennell/Bruce Coleman Ltd: Charles Henneghien/Bruce Coleman Ltd. 206 Ian Sansam. 207 David Attenborough. 208 Simon Trevor/Bruce Coleman Ltd. 209 Moser/Tayler/Alan Hutchison: J. Puttkamer/Alan Hutchison. 210 French Government Tourist Office. 211 David Attenborough. 212 David Attenborough. 213 Jean-Paul Ferrero/Ardea London: David Attenborough. 214 D. Baglin/N.H.P.A. 215 Warren and Genny Garst/Tom Stack & Associates. 216 Ronald Sheridan: Colin Maher.